CHRISTIANITY
AND CIVIL SOCIETY

THE ROCKWELL LECTURE SERIES
WERNER H. KELBER, GENERAL EDITOR

The Rockwell Lectures constitute the oldest designated and now endowed lecture series at Rice University, Houston, Texas. Since 1938, when the inaugural lecture was delivered, the Rockwell Fund has generously supported the series. The lectures are dedicated to the general subject of religion.

In the series:

Beyond Liberalism and Fundamentalism
by Nancey Murphy

Christianity and Civil Society
by Robert Wuthnow

CHRISTIANITY AND CIVIL SOCIETY

The Contemporary Debate

Robert Wuthnow

TRINITY PRESS INTERNATIONAL
VALLEY FORGE, PENNSYLVANIA

Trinity Press International, P.O. Box 851, Valley Forge, PA 19482-0851
Trinity Press International is part of the Morehouse Publishing Group.

Library of Congress Cataloging-in-Publication Data

Wuthnow, Robert.
    Christianity and civil society : the contemporary debate / Robert
Wuthnow.
        p.   cm. — (The Rockwell lectures : 1996)
    Includes bibliographical references and index.
    ISBN 1-56338-175-3 (cloth : alk. paper)
    1. Church and state—United States—History—20th century.
2. Church and social problems—United States—History—20th century.
3. United States—Church history—20th century.   4. United States—
Politics and government—20th century.   I. Title.   II. Series
BR516.W88   1996
261.7'0973—dc20   96-42499
                                                                              CIP
                    Ediset by Joan Marie Laflamme
                    Printed in the United States of America

96 97 98 99 00 01 02 7 6 5 4 3 2 1

To Sara

Contents

The Civil-Society Debate

In recent years, questions about civil society have been reopened with increasing urgency. How can we preserve and protect democracy? Is it possible to bring a moral dimension back into public life? How strong or weak do we want government to be? What can motivate us to be better, more responsibly engaged citizens? A few years ago, one would probably have needed to be a political science major to read anything about civil society.[1] Now it is scarcely possible to open the morning's newspaper without reading about the problems of civil society; indeed, one on-line news service showed more articles mentioning civil society in the past two years than in the entire decade before that.[2]

Religious groups have been in the forefront of efforts to address questions about civil society. Quietly and behind the scenes, clergy and laity have participated in forums to discuss violence, racism, and inequality in their communities, and they have participated in task forces and served on community councils concerned with AIDS, homelessness, child abuse, care of the elderly, and other serious social issues. More visibly, questions have been raised about the place of religion in schoolrooms and in the public square.

---

1. Especially helpful for understanding the civil society debate in the scholarly literature is Jean L. Cohen and Andrew Arato, *Civil Society and Political Theory* (Cambridge, Mass.: MIT Press, 1992); also of value are the essays in *Civil Society: Theory, History, Comparison*, ed. John A. Hall (London: Polity Press, 1995).

2. A Lexis-Nexis search of news articles found thirty-seven hundred containing the phrase "civil society" during 1994 and 1995, compared to twenty-nine hundred between 1985 and 1994.

1

An entire generation of intellectual work has now focused on the relationships between religion and politics, and especially between church and state, which have been brought into question by court cases, activist groups, and public officials eager to capitalize on the controversies surrounding these relationships. These controversies, such as the issue of voluntary prayer in schools, the teaching of creationism, and the role of conservative Christian leaders in politics, will continue to generate interest.

But it is time for a broader perspective to be taken. The civil-society debate is not ultimately about preachers in politics or even about First Amendment freedoms; it is about the quality of social life itself, especially in those voluntary realms governed by freedom of association rather than by the coercive powers of law and politics, and in those spheres of life motivated by commitments other than profit and self-interest. The civil-society debate is vitally concerned with the extent and quality of social interaction, with relationships that build and sustain moral commitment and character, and with the collective values that implicitly or explicitly define us as a people.

There are a number of reasons why the civil-society debate has arisen with such force in these closing years of the twentieth century, one of the most important of which is the struggle for democracy among the new nations of Eastern Europe. In the aftermath of Soviet communism, many of these nations have had to rebuild civil society virtually from scratch, initiating voluntary associations that had been eliminated under Stalinist oppression and teaching a new generation the responsibilities of citizenship. Discussions of civil society in the United States have benefited by the mirror provided by these efforts in Eastern Europe, just as they have to a lesser extent by political changes in Latin America and in Africa.

There are also larger, historical reasons for the renewed debate about civil society. The case can probably be made, for example, that the growth of strong national states was a distinct development in the history of the modern West, contingent on the spread of industry, the rise of national markets, technological innovations that increased the destructive potential of weapons, and labor movements that helped promote the creation of political parties. It could also be argued that national states reached their apex around the time of World War II, having risen in centralized power and been engaged almost continuously in large-scale wars from at least the time of Napoleon, and that the Cold War between the United States and the Soviet Union was simply an extension of the national rivalries that had developed during this period. Strong states lasted as long as they did because they helped to promote markets and in many cases helped to increase the quality of life for the average worker; yet there was also a high price to pay, both in taxation and in authoritarian control of society.[3] After the oil embargo in 1973, a general slowdown occurred in the economic growth of most industrial societies, sinking to less than 2 percent increases per year in most cases, compared to rates of 3 to 5 percent during the preceding two decades. Slower growth, along with more extensive integration of the global market itself, made it harder for national states to secure the income they needed or to play the role they formerly did in protecting national markets. The result was the collapse of the Soviet Union and the Eastern European states that had been part of the Warsaw pact. Simultaneously, economic stagnation in Western Europe and the United States mobilized sentiment to cut back on government programs and to devolve more of the activities of government to the local level and to voluntary associations.

The role of religion has been a central aspect of the civil-society debate, if for no other reason than the fact that churches, synagogues, and other places of worship have played a vital role in efforts to rebuild and maintain voluntary bases of self-government. In Russia, for example, new converts to the Orthodox church have been struggling to rebuild civil society on a parish basis from the bottom up, and, if their efforts are proving successful, then the statistics are at least heartening because 30 percent of Russians age 18 to 25 have become Christians since 1988 and the number of churches in Moscow alone has quadrupled in this period.[4] Elsewhere, Orthodox, Catholic, Lutheran, and other Protestant churches are seizing the initiative to recapture their earlier places of prominence in civil society. The opportunity to do so has also generated religious conflict. In Croatia, for example, the Croatian Democratic Union came into being as a result of free elections in 1989, and posters went up in shop

---

3. Charles Tilly, "Globalization Threatens Labor's Rights," *International Labor and Working-Class History* 47 (Spring 1995), 1-23.

4. Nathaniel Davis, *A Long Walk to Church: A Contemporary History of Russian Orthodoxy* (Boulder, Colo.: Westview Press, 1995).

windows all over the country declaring "God Protects Croatia." Yet within a few years, even as the country celebrated the twelve-hundredth anniversary of the coming of Christianity to the region, Catholics, Orthodox, and Muslims were killing each other (ten thousand dying in 1992 alone), and it was unclear whether a civil society could be built fast enough to spare the republic from ethnoreligious factionalism. In Zagreb, scholars and community leaders worked feverishly to find common ground, realizing that democracy was something that needed to be learned rather than simply declared.[5]

The relationship between Christianity and civil society has also been brought forcibly to attention by recent developments in Latin America, where some forty million of the continent's population are now Protestant and where Catholic membership is declining precipitously (as many as ten thousand abandoning their church every day in Brazil alone).[6] Many religious leaders there, Protestant and Catholic alike, are hopeful that Christianity can be a spiritual and ethical force in the formation of a new civilization that will be more democratic and economically vibrant. Yet fears are also voiced about growing numbers of violent confrontations between Catholics and Protestants, about the proliferation of new religious movements, and about alliances between conservative Protestants and dictatorial regimes.

In the United States, anti-government sentiment, tax-payer revolts, and diminishing revenues for government programs have prompted politicians and political analysts to call for greater efforts on the part of churches and other voluntary associations to fill the gap. "When Leviathan falters, civil society stirs," Michael Novak has written. And "when Leviathan relaxes, civil society expands." Americans have grown weary of government doing everything, Novak argues. We are a free people who want to do things for ourselves. In his view, civil society can only be saved by rolling back government and bringing voluntary efforts to center stage. "My proposal," he writes, "is that we must devolve the many functions now gathered up into the underachieving hands of the 'mommy state' back to the institutions of civil society—the family, the neighborhood, the local school (private when

---

5. Paul Mojzes, *Yugoslavia Inferno: Ethnoreligious Warfare in the Balkans* (New York: Continuum, 1994).

6. Eugene L. Stockwell, "Open and Closed: Protestantism in Latin America," *Christian Century* (March 22, 1995), 317.

and wherever possible), the local church, and the variety of local associations. We must restore the practices of self-government as well as the public ideal of civic republican virtues."[7] One does not have to agree with Novak's specific political orientations to recognize that the sentiment he describes is a powerful tradition in American culture.

One important aspect of the recent debate over the role of religion in civil society is that all sorts of new proposals for bringing religion back into the public life of our nation are being tried, some of which take bizarre forms and most of which receive mixed reviews. For example, the state of Arkansas has been experimenting the past few years with something called Christian Heritage Week, which is sandwiched between National Canned Foods Month and Secretary's Day and overlaps with Thai Heritage Month and National Anxiety Month. Its supporters conceived it as a tactful way of bringing Christianity into the public square, but critics worry that religion will become a kind of aesthetic experience, like touring the great cathedrals of Europe, or simply be dragged down by the drumrolls and platitudes of all government projects.[8] As this example suggests, the civil-society debate poses dangers for religion, as well as opportunities.

The civil-society debate also challenges received wisdom about the trajectory of religion in modern societies. A generation ago, many social scientists subscribed to a version of modernization theory that viewed the modern, liberal conception of civil society as a natural extension of Christianity, arguing that such principles as liberty and equality, for example, were really biblical values that had simply been extracted from their earlier dependence on Christian theology. Recent scholarship has become more critical of that view, placing more emphasis on conflict and historical discontinuity and seeing in writers such as Spinoza, Hobbes, and Locke a bitter struggle against Christianity in the name of secular, democratic ideals.[9] In recognizing that the liberal conception of civil society was developed in opposition to Christianity, this recent scholarship also opens the way, how-

---

7. Michael Novak, "The Conservative Mood," *Society* 31 (January 1994), 13.

8. Paul Greenberg, "Celebrate: Take a Christian to Lunch," *Memphis Commercial Appeal* (February 10, 1995), 9A.

9. Adam Wolfson, "The Empire of Fashion," *Public Interest* (March 22, 1995), 111.

ever, to paying greater attention to the continuing conflicts between the two, especially in societies like the United States where Christianity has remained strong. If separation of church and state provided the means of keeping religious conflicts at bay, for example, then the lingering question is whether such separation also excludes valuable sources of public opinion on which democratic government itself may depend.

For present purposes, the historical connections between Christianity and civil society can be dispensed with, rather than detouring into their complexities, by noting only that the principles of Christianity, however favorable to civil society they may have been, were always worked out in a social context that channeled them in a variety of directions. Thus, it is reasonable to argue, as James Luther Adams did a generation ago, or as Max Stackhouse has more recently, that the birth of a modern notion of civil society was furthered by the sectarian diversity that emerged in Europe following the Protestant Reformation and that often created factions distrustful of a strong state.[10] To the extent that North America was settled by Europeans from these dissenting traditions, civil society in the United States may also be said to have benefited from Christianity. At the same time, it is worth emphasizing that Christian principles of order, justice, mercy, and companionship were also deeply implicated in regimes such as Catholic Spain or Lutheran Sweden in which civil society followed a very different course than in the United States, and that Christianity was often the source of militant movements that had to be tamed by constitutional reforms before what we know as civil society in its modern form could emerge. To insist that Christianity always has a healthy influence on civil society because it is true or good or humanitarian, therefore, is to ride roughshod over the difficult terrain of social reality, and the contemporary debate is no exception: civil society might be strengthened if there were more or better Christianity, but it also might not be, and the difference

---

10. James Luther Adams, *Voluntary Associations: Socio-Cultural Analyses and Theological Interpretation*, ed. J. Ronald Engel (Chicago: Explorations Press, 1986); Max L. Stackhouse, "Religion and the Social Space for Voluntary Institutions," in *Faith and Philanthropy in America*, ed. Robert Wuthnow and Virginia A. Hodgkinson (San Francisco: Jossey Bass, 1990).

would depend largely on the organizational and political circumstances under which Christianity was put into practice.[11]

In short, the relationship between Christianity and civil society is a question that must be approached empirically, focusing on the complex realities of American society at the end of the twentieth century, rather than extrapolating from abstract theories or historical arguments. The importance of examining this relationship nevertheless derives from the fact that civil society is widely regarded as a normative good, as a desirable dimension of social life that is worth preserving. It is so because moral values and a sense of personal integrity and civic responsibility are generally regarded as part of the formula for a good society, but legislation is a blunt instrument for shaping people's behavior; thus, we look to families, schools, churches, and community organizations to instill values. The other reason is that civil society is always positioned between the government and the individual, guarding the sanctity of individual freedoms against government intrusion but also linking individuals with one another so that they can work effectively with the state.[12]

Civil society is thus the arena in which individual freedoms, even those that are self-interested, are kept in tension with collective values and community participation. In recognizing the inevitability of this tension, the civil-society debate is thus, in my view, preferable to the emphasis one finds in many circles on questions of community. The trouble with *community* is that its scope is seldom specified, leaving readers to wonder whether they are being exposed to arguments about neighborhoods, as literal geographic communities in particular places, or national societies, or the entire planet, or some other social designation, such as the African-American community, the Christian community, the community of nations, or communities of memory. Community is often problematic as well because the very

---

11. An especially good treatment of the historical origins of the current civil-society debate is that of Adam B. Seligman, *The Idea of Civil Society* (New York: Free Press, 1992); see also Iswan Hont and Michael Ignatieff, eds., *Wealth and Virtue: The Shaping of Political Economy in the Scottish Enlightenment* (Cambridge: Cambridge University Press, 1984); John Keane, ed., *Civil Society and the State: New European Perspectives* (London: Verso, 1988).

12. Ernest Gellner, *Conditions of Liberty: Civil Society and Its Rivals* (London: Penguin, 1994), includes much on the normative value of civil society.

characteristics it is supposed to represent—responsibility, interaction, mutuality, a common spirit—are often lacking. For example, a neighborhood might fall far short of the idea of community if that idea was meant to include affectional bonds among inhabitants who actually knew each other and interacted on a regular basis. In contrast, civil society is generally understood to include neighborhoods, voluntary associations, and the like, but these components may or may not be appropriately described as communities.

Civil society is also a preferable concept to community because the latter pays virtually no attention to the role of government, including law, whereas civil society is one of those relational constructs that has meaning only in relation to government. That is, community has a kind of horizontal connotation in which it is presumed that people in nearly equal circumstances govern themselves largely on the basis of moral virtue and altruistic sentiments; in comparison, civil society is understood to include a variety of organizations that may well be in tension with one another and whose coexistence depends on a framework of shared legal understandings, and whose activities are inevitably concerned with gaining power for themselves and their causes by petitioning government. This means, incidentally, that it should not be surprising to find the member groups of civil society, even those that are most opposed to a powerful government, making political appeals and engaging in the political process. Civil society is public in precisely this sense: it is concerned with the common good, one important aspect of which is the distribution of power.

The scholarly literature continues to debate the meaning of civil society: some take Hegel's definition, which includes in civil society virtually everything that is not officially part of the state; others define civil society more specifically to exclude not only the coercive mechanisms of government but also the marketplace or economic sector and those aspects of personal life, including much of what takes place within families, that are strictly up to the individual. But by any definition, voluntary associations are an important part of civil society, especially in the United States, as Tocqueville pointed out more than a century ago, and churches, along with other religious organizations, are thus an inescapable feature of civil society.[13]

---

13. On some of the varying views of civil society, see the essays in *Between States and Markets*, ed. Robert Wuthnow (Princeton: Princeton University Press, 1991).

In the pages that follow, I consider three aspects of the relationship between Christianity and civil society. In chapter 1, my focus is on the question of whether civil society is in jeopardy, and I pay special attention to the influence of Christianity, asking whether or not this influence is declining and, if so, what the effects on civil society may be. In chapter 2, I focus on the question of whether or not Christians can be civil, examining the conflicts that have arisen among religious groups in the public arena, including the so-called culture wars that many in the media have been discussing. And in the final chapter, I examine the growing multiculturalism of civil society in the United States, asking how Christian groups are responding to the new diversity and considering how Christianity can regain a critical voice for itself in these debates.

I should note that I emphasize Christianity here chiefly in the interest of honesty, for that is what I know best. Yet much of what I have to say, I suspect, applies to other U.S. religions as well. My perspective is that of a social scientist, although I am also a practitioner of Christianity, and thus my hope is to stimulate thinking about civil society that may be of value for academicians and religious leaders alike.

Is Civil Society in Jeopardy?

In the United States today, there is a widespread—and growing—impression that the moorings of civil society are becoming perilously weak. Public officials from all points of the political spectrum have voiced this concern, as have a large number of social scientists. In a recent speech to the National Press Club, New Jersey's Democratic senator Bill Bradley described civil society as "the sphere of our most basic humanity," the "everyday realm that is governed by values such as responsibility, trust, fraternity, solidarity, and love," but, Bradley went on to say, civil society is no longer as strong as it once was, especially because civic associations are failing to attract the involvement of ordinary citizens. "Like fish floating on the surface of a polluted river," Bradley observed, "the network of voluntary associations in America seems to be dying."[1] Picking up the same theme in a published interview, Hillary Rodham Clinton argued that "the 'intermediary institutions' in civil society—the family, the church, the neighborhood associations—are key [to a strong society], and they have really broken down in the last [few] decades."[2] Similar sentiments have been expressed in other quarters as well. In a recent edition of *Policy Review*, foundation official William Schambra writes that "civil society's decline [is] evident throughout our daily life," and he lists "soaring rates of crime, divorce, illegitimacy, neighborhood deterioration, welfare dependency, chemical addiction, suicide, and virtu-

---

1. Senator Bill Bradley, "National Press Club Luncheon Speaker," *Federal News Service* (February 9, 1995), n.p.
2. Quoted in Ann Pleshette Murphy, "An Exclusive Interview with Chelsea's Parents," *Parents' Magazine* (May 1994), 22.

ally every other indicator of pathology" as evidence.[3] The same litany was the subject of John Silber's 1995 commencement address at Boston University, in which he spoke of a crisis of spirit threatening to engulf America. Counseling listeners that neither law nor economic prosperity could save them, Silber called for a new moral commitment grounded in "honor and truth and in the essential role of duty and obligation in our lives."[4]

The current hand wringing about civil society is not limited to public officials or social analysts; most ordinary Americans also sense that something has gone wrong with our society. Erosion of the moral values on which any good society depends is an ailment widely perceived to be plaguing the nation. For instance, one national survey found that 63 percent of the public thought the "United States is in a moral decline"; another poll documented that 68 percent of the public were dissatisfied with the honesty and ethical standards of their fellow Americans; and in yet another poll, 69 percent of the public acknowledged that they themselves believed "there are few moral absolutes."[5]

It is not hard to understand why civil society appears to be in jeopardy. To live in harmony as citizens who trust one another and who feel responsible to uphold the democratic traditions on which society is based requires, above all, that people feel safe enough to venture out of their houses, to travel along the city streets to work or to their places of worship, and to feel that the fruits of their labors will be rewarded. Yet we live in a society where one-quarter of the population is victimized by crime every year (in urban areas this proportion rises to 30 percent).[6] One person in twenty is a victim of violent crime, such as rape, robbery, or assault, and one in five is a

---

3. William A. Schambra, "The Old Values of the New Citizenship," *Policy Review* (Summer 1994), 32.

4. John Silber, "Obedience to the Unenforceable," Commencement Address, Boston University, May 21, 1995.

5. "Are We Witnessing a Resurgence of Moral Absolutes?" *Emerging Trends* (January 1995), 1-2; figures in the text are all from Gallup surveys conducted between 1991 and 1994.

6. U.S. Bureau of the Census, *Statistical Abstract of the United States: 1992* (112th edition). Washington, D.C.: U.S. Government Printing Office, 1992), 186.

victim of theft or burglary. Whether it is experienced personally or not, crime and the publicity surrounding it have become so familiar that few Americans feel safe, especially in the nation's major cities. In fact, more than five-sixths of the public considers New York an unsafe place to live; at least two-thirds of the public believes the same concerning Miami, Washington D.C., Detroit, Chicago, and Los Angeles.[7]

If the family is the heart of civil society—anchoring people in loving relationships that give them self-confidence and social skills and that encourage them to trust and to work with others for the good of their own and their children's futures—then it is also clear why civil society appears to be in serious trouble. Sociologist Andrew Cherlin has tracked the enormous changes that have overtaken the American family by comparing marriage and divorce statistics for older and younger Americans. For those born in the early decades of this century, Cherlin shows, the chances of marrying were better than 90 percent and the chances of divorce were approximately 20 percent; in contrast, for people born around 1970, the chances of marrying are still almost 90 percent, but the chances of divorce are about 45 percent.[8]

Apart from the emotional trauma generated for individual spouses, high rates of divorce mean that approximately a quarter of American children are being reared by a single parent, often quite effectively but without many of the social and economic resources needed to give them the best opportunities to succeed in life. As a recent book by Sara McLanahan and Gary Sandefur has shown, children from single-parent families are more likely to drop out of high school, less likely to succeed academically in high school and college, and more likely to suffer from low self-esteem than children from two-parent families, even when differences in other factors are taken into account.[9]

---

7. George Gallup, Jr., and Frank Newport, "Major U.S. Cities Seen as Unsafe Places to Live and Work," *The Gallup Poll* (September 19, 1990), 1.

8. Andrew J. Cherlin, *Marriage, Divorce, Remarriage,* rev. ed. (Cambridge, Mass.: Harvard University Press, 1992).

9. Sara McLanahan and Gary Sandefur, *Growing Up with a Single Parent: What Hurts, What Helps* (Cambridge, Mass.: Harvard University Press, 1994).

Civil society depends to a great extent on learning civility, including trust and respect, in the home. Yet it is clear that civil society is not as healthy as it should be when growing numbers of children are abused by their parents and step-parents. According to government statistics, the number of children in the United States who were abused or maltreated tripled between 1976 and 1986 alone, and unofficial estimates of child neglect and abuse run much higher.[10]

It is surprising that after experiencing mistreatment at home and witnessing countless acts of violence on television and in motion pictures, American young people are not more prone to incivility than they are. The music of Snoop Doggy Dogg, gangsta rap, grunge rock, and heavy metal is but one indication of such incivility. Abusive language, a proliferation of four-letter words in the mass media, and a decline in etiquette and public decorum all point to the growth of incivility. What do we make of the MTV town meeting in 1994 at which Letitia Thompson of Potomac, Maryland, asked President Clinton whether he wore briefs or boxers? Is this simply a move of solidarity between the populace and public leaders, or does it signal a worrisome breakdown of respect and decorum? And, lest incivility be viewed only as an aspect of being young, we should remind ourselves that analysts of recent electoral campaigns have also complained of the growing incivility in this arena, consisting of mean-spirited discourse intent on winning at all cost, even if it means character assassination, half lies, and the witless portrayal of violence. One may not agree with his politics, but William Bennett clearly had a point when he remarked recently, "We have become the kind of society that civilized countries used to send missionaries to."[11]

CIVIC PARTICIPATION

The difficulty with arguments that focus entirely on street violence, X-rated language, teenage pregnancy, and other social ills is that these conditions can readily be dismissed as *someone else's* problems—the

---

10. *U.S. Statistical Abstract*, 186.

11. Quoted in William F. Buckley, Jr., "Let Us Pray? The Link between Excessive Church-State Prohibitions and the US's Increasing Problems," *National Review* 19 (October 10, 1994), 86.

fault of Hollywood producers or big government or, worse, certain neighborhoods, income groups, or racial minorities presumed to be deficient in socially uplifting virtues. Complaints about the demise of civility can be dismissed on grounds that these are the nitpicky concerns of affluent and powerful middle-class Americans who are unwilling to do anything serious about working for justice and equity. As a participant at one conference on the subject asserted, "People of principle lament the collapse of decorum and simultaneously vote themselves annual pension subsidies and tax exemptions in the tens of billions of dollars—funds that build terraced perches, in country clubs and elsewhere, from which to observe and discuss the decline of values."[12] A more penetrating critique of civil society has thus come from social observers worried about the decline of civic-mindedness among the American majority itself.

One of the most provocative of such critiques in recent years is that of Harvard political scientist Robert Putnam. Drawing on Tocqueville, as well as on a previous study of his own in which he examined the effects of associations on democracy in Italy, Putnam argues that civic engagement is not only essential to American democracy, but that it has also been declining significantly in recent decades. Surveying a wide variety of evidence, Putnam suggests that the following kinds of civic participation have all eroded: voter turnout has declined by approximately one-quarter since the early 1960s, attendance at public meetings on town or school affairs has dropped by a third since 1973, daily newspaper readership has fallen by a quarter since 1970, membership in labor unions has plummeted by more than half since 1975, participation in parent-teacher associations is only about half what it was in 1964, membership in Boy Scouts is off 26 percent since 1970, Red Cross participation is down 61 percent since 1970, regular involvement in volunteer work is about a sixth lower than in 1974, and membership in fraternal organizations, such as Lions, Elks, and Shriners, has declined by nearly 40 percent since the 1950s. On the matter of greatest interest to the

---

12. Benjamin DeMott at a White House Conference on "Character Building for a Democratic, Civil Society," quoted in Paul Galloway, "Year in Religion: Full of Politics, Protests, Priests and Death," *Charleston Gazette* (December 31, 1994), P2B.

present discussion, Putnam concludes that "net participation by Americans [in religious organizations], both in religious services and in church-related groups, has modestly declined (by perhaps a fifth) since the 1960s." He also observes, on a more whimsical note, that participation in team bowling has decreased by 40 percent since 1980, despite the fact that overall participation in bowling has increased, thus leading to the melancholy conclusion that more Americans are bowling alone.[13]

Putnam's paper was circulated widely before it was published, becoming required reading at the White House and playing an influential role in President Clinton's State of the Union speech in January 1995, which concluded with an endorsement of AmeriCorps volunteers and a plea for more Americans to become involved in civic affairs. Almost immediately, Putnam's paper also came under attack for presenting a one-sided view of American life. Critics pointed out that Americans were in fact bowling with friends and neighbors, even if league bowling was sinking in popularity. They also cautioned that volunteerism should not be underemphasized and suggested that some indicators of civic involvement were on the rise. As one article counseled: "There are strong signs that Americans' social engagement, far from sinking on down, is already rebounding."[14]

To his credit, Putnam has elevated the civil-society debate to a new level, focusing our attention away from the crime and incivility that so often occupy the attention of journalists and causing us to think more deeply about what he calls social capital—all the relationships and interpersonal skills, such as "networks, norms, and social trust, that facilitate coordination and cooperation for mutual benefit."[15]

---

13. Robert D. Putnam, "Bowling Alone: America's Declining Social Capital," *Journal of Democracy* 6 (January 1995), 65-78. My discussion is based on a revised version of "Bowling Alone: Democracy in America at the End of the Twentieth Century," unpublished paper presented at the Nobel Symposium on Democracy's Victory and Crisis, Uppsala, Sweden, March 1995 draft. I am grateful to Professor Putnam for sending me a copy of this paper.

14. "The Solitary Bowler," *Economist* (February 18, 1995), 21; see also, Leslie Lenkowski, "Are We Still a Nation of Joiners?" (draft manuscript provided to me by the author).

15. Ibid., 6.

As Tocqueville did a century and a half ago, Putnam recognizes that civic engagement is a pivotal form of social capital. Because it is voluntary, civic engagement draws on personal commitment and thus brings considerations of moral virtue into public life. Because it is local, it gives individuals a sense that they can make a difference in their communities. And because it is social, civic engagement demonstrates that even individual needs are best pursued in the company of others.

Also like Tocqueville, Putnam recognizes the importance of religion as a kind of social capital that can contribute to the strength of civil society. Local congregations are the places in which people learn to interact with and trust one another, gaining the interpersonal skills needed to participate in other civic organizations and developing the networks on which jobs, support groups, and vital information about public events may depend. Whatever their specific teachings, congregations forge important social bonds in all these ways. Indeed, Putnam cites as evidence an intriguing study by Anne Case and Lawrence Katz of disadvantaged youths in Boston showing that having *neighbors* who attend church was a critical factor, taking into account all the individual characteristics of the youths themselves, in youths having jobs, being less likely to use drugs, and being less likely to engage in criminal activity.[16] Anecdotal evidence supporting this finding is readily available. Not only do churches provide networks for disadvantaged youths, but they also mobilize much of the effort to operate soup kitchens and homeless shelters and to provide other services in decaying neighborhoods. As Glenn Loury has observed, "The reports of successful efforts at reconstruction in ghetto communities invariably reveal a religious institution, or a set of devout believers, at the center of the effort."[17]

The wider potential of religion is also evident in public perceptions of how to deal with community problems. One survey asked people to think about "the problems facing your city or local community" and to say how much confidence they had in various institutions' ability to

---

16. Anne C. Case and Lawrence F. Katz, "The Company You Keep: The Effects of Family and Neighborhood on Disadvantaged Youths" (Cambridge, Mass.: National Bureau of Economic Research, 1991), NBER Working Paper No. 3705.

17. Quoted in Schambra, "The Old Values of the New Citizenship."

deal with these problems. In response 57 percent said they had a great deal or a lot of confidence in churches and synagogues for dealing with such problems, followed by 54 percent who said this about other volunteer groups; in comparison, fewer than one-third of the public expressed this much confidence in local businesses, local government, state and federal government, or political parties.[18]

The fact that Putnam's statistics suggest a decline in the strength of American religion, however, raises the question of whether Christianity's contribution to civil society is as strong as it once was. Indeed, it is this question to which I want to pay particular attention. America's churches have never been the sole source of social capital on which civil society depends, but they have certainly been one of the most important sources of civic engagement, drawing millions of people into congregations where they could become acquainted with their neighbors and instilling a sense of civic responsibility that often resulted in voter registration drives, social protest movements, and campaigns to help the poor and the needy. Yet there is a longstanding theoretical perspective in the social sciences suggesting that American society is becoming increasingly secularized. Whether or not one happens to be a Christian, a decline in the strength of organized religion could thus signal a weakening of civil society itself.

THE DECLINE OF RELIGION?

What do we know about American religion? Is it declining, or isn't it? When the omnipresent Gallup poll-takers go out to answer this question, here are some of the things they find:

- 69 percent of the American public are members of a church or synagogue, only 4 percent fewer than were members sixty years ago.[19]

---

18. "Churches Rated Best Able to Deal with Local Community Problems," *Emerging Trends* (December 1990), 3-4.

19. "Church Membership Continues to Show Remarkable Stability," *Emerging Trends* (March 1995), 1; "Religion in America, 50 Years: 1935-1985," *The Gallup Report* (May 1985), No. 236. The earlier figure for church membership was 73 percent in 1937; a high of 76 percent was recorded in 1947; and a low of 67 percent was recorded in 1981.

- 40 percent claim to have attended church or synagogue in the last seven days, virtually the same percentage as in 1939.[20]
- Over the past five decades, no Gallup poll has found fewer than 94 percent of the public claiming they believe in God.[21]

Now, it is true that figures like these can be misleading. For example, the figures on church attendance have been challenged by researchers who actually visited churches in several areas, counting cars in church parking lots on Sunday mornings and collecting attendance records from pastors. This research concluded that perhaps as few as 20 percent of the public attends religious services on a given weekend.[22] We also know from surveys that far less of the public than the 94 percent who claim to believe in God actually feel certain that God exists or have personally felt close to God. But there is no evidence that doubt and distance from God have increased in recent years.

Other surveys show that prayer remains an active part of American life, as does belief in an afterlife.[23] Religious giving is high, comprising about half of all charitable giving of all kinds, and so is volunteer effort donated to religious organizations.[24] And all these manifestations of religious commitment remain much higher in the United States than in any other industrial nation.[25] Moreover, it is

20. "Church Attendance Unchanged as We Enter the 1990s," *Emerging Trends* (June 1990), 4.

21. "50 Years of Gallup Polls Find Nearly Everybody Believes in God," *Emerging Trends* (January 1995), 5; according to this report, 96 percent of the adult public in 1994 said yes when asked, "Do you believe in God, or a universal spirit?" This was the same percentage as in 1944.

22. C. Kirk Hadaway, Penny Long Marler, and Mark Chaves, "What the Polls Don't Show: A Closer Look at U.S. Church Attendance," *American Sociological Review* 58 (December 1993), 741-52; for a counterargument, see "Do That Many People Really Attend Worship Services?" *Emerging Trends* (May 1994), 1-3.

23. "Saying Grace Before Meals Still a Common Practice," *Emerging Trends* (May 1994), 2; Margaret M. Poloma and George H. Gallup, Jr., *Varieties of Prayer: A Survey Report* (Philadelphia: Trinity Press International, 1991).

24. Virginia A. Hodgkinson and Murray S. Weitzman, *Giving and Volunteering in the United States: Findings from a National Survey, 1994 Edition* (Washington, D.C.: Independent Sector, 1994).

25. Kenneth D. Wald, *Religion and Politics in the United States* (New York: St. Martin's Press, 1987), ch. 1.

not just the penchant of Gallup pollsters to demonstrate such results. Catholic sociologist Andrew Greeley, drawing on surveys conducted by the University of Chicago, has been arguing for some time that there is no secularization in the United States; indeed, Greeley states categorically that "if a secularization dynamic is at work in the United States, it is invisible to all the measures of religion which survey takers have been using for at least twenty years and in many cases for fifty years."[26] Several community studies, carefully retracing the steps of anthropologists more than fifty years ago, have also concluded that religion is as strong now as it was then.[27]

Judging from the wider range of information available about religious trends, then, one would have to conclude that Robert Putnam is wrong as far as the decline of religion is concerned. Indeed, his analysis appears to be flawed by having taken an arbitrarily high point—during the 1950s—as his baseline for making comparisons. As most observers recognized, even at the time, the 1950s witnessed a temporary resurgence of piety, partly because congregations were rebuilding after a lull imposed by the Great Depression and World War II, perhaps partly because of fears generated by the Cold War, and probably in large measure because of the burgeoning number of families with young children. But trends over a longer period, as well as during roughly the past twenty years, have been relatively flat.

Not only does such evidence suggest that Putnam may be wrong about religion, but by implication, it also reinforces the possibility, suggested by his critics, that the other data on which his conclusions about civic decline are based may be revealing only part of the picture. For example, the number of neighborhood crimewatch groups grew from 10,000 in 1970 to 150,000 in 1992, when they represented approximately thirty million people.[28] Many other associations, such as political-action committees and special-interest groups, have risen in numbers as well, perhaps taking the place of organizations, such as fraternal orders and labor unions, which Putnam finds are declining. It may well be, of course, that these newer organiza-

---

26. Andrew Greeley, "The Persistence of Religion," *Cross Currents* (Spring 1995), 32-33.

27. Theodore Caplow, Howard M. Bahr, and Bruce A. Chadwick, *All Faithful People: Change and Continuity in Middletown's Religion* (Minneapolis: University of Minnesota Press, 1983).

28. "The Solitary Bowler."

tions do not meet the criteria of creating social capital, especially if members never attend meetings and simply send in subscription dues once a year. Nevertheless, other voluntary-association activity is clearly more robust than Putnam acknowledges. For example, his evidence on the decline in volunteering is taken from limited data collected in surveys for the U.S. Labor Department; more extensive data, however, suggests little decline in volunteering and perhaps even an increase in overall prosocial behavior of this kind. For instance, in national surveys asking, "Do you, yourself, happen to be involved in any charity or social service activities, such as helping the poor, the sick, or the elderly?" figures rose from 26 percent in 1977 to 29 percent in 1981, to 36 percent in 1986, and then to 41 percent in 1989, the last time the question was asked.[29] A somewhat different question, used in 1991, found that 38 percent of the public claimed to have increased the amount of time they spent volunteering for charity or social-service activities in the past five years, while only 8 percent had decreased this amount of time.[30] Other evidence, collected by Independent Sector, indicates that volunteering was virtually constant as a percentage of the adult public between 1987 and 1993, and that it was not sporadic, averaging in excess of four hours per week per volunteer, and that most of it took place in conjunction with other people working together in formal voluntary associations.[31]

All this should be reassuring. As far as social capital is concerned, there is at least little indication that religious commitment is any less prominent in our society than it ever was. Indeed, Putnam's own figures suggest that religious involvement has been more stable than most other kinds of civic engagement. Only the churlish academic would keep on asking questions. But that is precisely what we need to do, for the impact of Christianity on civil society cannot be gauged by arguments about social capital alone.

A generation ago, Will Herberg, in his widely read book *Protestant-Catholic-Jew*, suggested that American religion was perhaps con-

---

29. Gallup surveys, as reported on Public Opinion Online, a service of the Roper Center at the University of Connecticut.

30. *The Gallup Poll* (April 7, 1991).

31. Virginia A. Hodgkinson, Heather A. Gorski, Stephen M. Noga, and E.. Knauft, *Giving and Volunteering in the United States, Vol. II: Trends in Giving and Volunteering by Type of Charity* (Washington, D.C.: Independent Sector, 1995).

tinent-wide but (like top soil) only a few inches thick. It was, he suggested, "customary," part of being a good American, to have faith.[32] But how deep was that faith? Did it reflect personal and spiritual maturity? Was it capable of sustaining life? Could it influence how people lived out their lives? Let us consider some additional evidence:

- In 1952, 75 percent of the American public said religion was very important in their lives; since the 1980s, that figure has been hovering around 55 percent. Surely a drop from three-quarters to half of the public who consider religion a salient value in their lives is significant.[33]
- In 1957, 81 percent of the American public thought religion provided answers to all or most of today's problems; by 1984, this figure had slipped to 56 percent.[34]
- In 1963, 65 percent of the American public said the Bible is the inspired word of God and should be taken literally, word for word; by 1978, that figure had slipped to 38 percent; and in 1992, only 32 percent of the public gave this response.[35] Of course most Americans still believe the Bible is divinely inspired, even if it does contain some errors; nevertheless, the proportion who regard the Bible simply as a book of fables and myths has grown from 11 percent in 1963 to 16 percent in 1992.

Other evidence also gives cause for concern. The declining strength of mainline Protestant denominations is by now well known. During the 1940s and 1950s, denominations such as the Episcopal, Presbyterian, and Methodist churches grew at about the same rate as the U.S. population. But since the 1960s, these denominations have lost between a quarter and a third of their members. Why? Largely because they were unable to retain their young people. And why was

---

32. Will Herberg, *Protestant-Catholic-Jew: An Essay in American Religious Sociology*, rev. ed. (New York: Anchor, 1960).

33. "The Importance of Religion Intensifies as People Grow Older," *Emerging Trends* (March 1995), 4-5; according to this report, 58 percent of the adult public said religion was very important to them in 1994.

34. "Religion in America, 50 Years: 1935-1985," 18.

35. "Literal Belief in the Bible Declining in U.S.," *Emerging Trends* (January 1992), 1.

this? According to a recent study of Presbyterians who went through confirmation classes in the 1960s, the main reason was theological: the church simply didn't teach them a clear, compelling set of religious beliefs.[36]

Indeed, the crisis in belief is readily documented in a wide variety of studies. Consider the following:

- In a 1991 study, only 31 percent of the public identified "scripture" as the most believable authority in matters of truth (in comparison, 43 percent listed "personal experience").[37]
- In the same study, 69 percent agreed that "there are few moral absolutes, what is right or wrong usually varies from situation to situation."[38]
- In one of the national surveys I conducted, 57 percent of the American labor force incorrectly identified Paul as one of the twelve disciples.[39]
- In the same survey, 25 percent incorrectly said the book of Acts is in the Old Testament.[40]
- And in a Gallup survey, only 37 percent of the public could name all four of the gospels.[41]

It may be that Herberg's characterization of American religion a generation ago is still apt: as a society, we are interested in it, and most of us have some connection with religious organizations of some kind. But it may not be soil that has been cultivated very well. Indeed, this is precisely the conclusion George Gallup came to a few years ago from reflecting on the results of his own research. "We believe in

---

36. Dean R. Hoge, Benton Johnson, and Donald A. Luidens, *Vanishing Boundaries: The Religion of Mainline Protestant Baby Boomers* (Louisville: Westminster/John Knox Press, 1994).

37. Robert Bezilla, *Religion in America, 1992-93* (Princeton: Princeton Religion Research Center, 1993), 23.

38. Ibid., 24.

39. Robert Wuthnow, *God and Mammon in America* (New York: Free Press, 1994).

40. Ibid.

41. George Gallup, Jr. and Frank Newport, "The Bible Is Still Widely Read and Studied, But Biblical Illiteracy Remains Widespread," *The Gallup Poll* (November 15, 1990), 1-2.

God," he wrote, "but this God is often only an affirming one, not a demanding one. . . . We pray but often in a desultory fashion, with the emphasis on asking. . . . We revere the Bible, but we don't read it. . . . We want the fruits of faith, but not the obligations."[42]

If the picture among adults is at best mixed, research among teenagers and on patterns of religious training suggests that religion may weaken further in the future. For example, one national survey of teenagers found that fewer than half regarded "having a deep religious faith" as being very important to them— about the same proportion as that valuing "having lots of money," and less than half as many as valued personal happiness and being well educated.[43] Another study, examining the child-rearing practices of baby boomers, found that only half were exposing their children to formal religious training of any kind, compared with 86 percent who themselves had received religious training as children. *Significant* exposure was even lower: only 34 percent were sending their children to Sunday school classes, whereas 63 percent had themselves attended such classes.[44]

It is also worth noting that many Americans—who sometimes serve better in surveys as observers of their neighbors than of themselves— *perceive* a decline in religion. For instance, one national survey showed that 58 percent felt "the number of people in America who take their religious faith seriously is . . . declining."[45] Another study found that 69 percent of the public thought "religion as a whole is . . . losing its influence" on American life, while only 27 percent said religion's influence was increasing.[46] And, whether or not religion is declining in absolute terms, many Americans are skeptical about the churches' ability to step in and solve social problems that government and pri-

---

42. George H. Gallup, Jr., "Looking Ahead to the Year 2000," in *Religion in America, 1990* (Princeton: Princeton Religion Research Center, 1990), 7.

43. "Having a Deep Religious Faith Ranked Comparatively Low by Teens," *Emerging Trends* (June 1990), 3.

44. Gallup Unchurched American Study, 1978; my analysis of persons age 18 through 34.

45. "Are People Taking Religion More Seriously?" *Emerging Trends* (January 1995), 3; the question also found that 37 percent thought this number was growing.

46. Lydia Saad and Leslie McAneny, "Most Americans Think Religion Losing Clout in the 1990s," *The Gallup Poll* (April 14, 1994), 1-4.

vate agencies have been unable to handle. For example, one poll found that only 25 percent of the public believed "private charitable institutions, churches, and community groups will be able to step in and make up for the government cutbacks," while 60 percent felt "those institutions [don't] have the resources to do that."[47]

That, in short, is one answer to the question of whether religion is declining. If Herberg was correct in arguing that American religion was shallow in the 1950s, it is probably safe to say that it is even shallower in the 1990s. And, if it is, civil society may be weakened in ways not fully captured by arguments about social capital. Mainline Protestant denominations were a significant source of political mobilization a generation ago, not only by drawing people into congregations, but also by uniting those congregations in federations, regionally and nationally, that could debate important social issues, render opinions on these issues, pay for lobbyists in the nation's capital, and organize clergy and laity for social causes. The civil rights movement, the protests against the Vietnam war, and the antinuclear movement were all important ways in which the mainline churches influenced civil society. Today, smaller memberships and tighter budgets make it harder for many denominations to participate effectively in such efforts.

Of course, liberal Protestants and Catholics may not be unhappy about some of the shifts that are evident in public opinion polls, such as the decline in biblical literalism. Indeed, leaders of these theologically liberal or moderate churches have probably worked to combat biblical literalism and moral absolutism in their congregations. From the standpoint of thinking about civil society, one might also argue that any shift from dogmatism toward relativism in religion should be viewed as a healthy development. Yet it is also true that churches do not exist simply to cultivate social capital and to discuss social issues. Dean Kelley demonstrated some years ago that churches were stronger when they made greater demands on their parishioners' lives than when they functioned as garden-variety social clubs.[48] If fewer

---

47. *Los Angeles Times* survey of 1,353 adults in the United States in January 1995.

48. Dean M. Kelley, *Why Conservative Churches Are Growing: A Study in the Sociology of Religion*, rev. ed. (Macon, Ga.: Mercer University Press, 1986).

and fewer people take religion seriously, then an erosion of church participation itself cannot be far behind.

THE PUBLIC ROLE OF RELIGION

But there is another way of addressing the question of Christianity and civil society. In fact, what I want to focus on mainly is the question of how much religious commitment influences the rest of our lives. Oxford sociologist Bryan Wilson, a scholar who has spent a lifetime considering the question of secularization, has written that the best definition of it is not the decline of religion itself, but the decline in religion's ability to influence other spheres of life.[49] That seems to me to be an important observation. We judge religion by its effects. The Bible itself teaches us to do this: "Ye are the salt of the earth." What good is the salt if it has lost its flavor? Indeed, this is what sets religion apart from most of the things social scientists study. We don't study attendance at the opera to see what effects it has on people's lives, but we do study religious attendance that way.

Influence is very different from the kinds of evidence I've presented thus far. For the vitality of civil society, a smaller number of religious activists could still make a big difference—perhaps the churches are becoming leaner and meaner. At least that has been the hope of some leaders of declining mainline denominations. For particular individuals, spirituality might not come out in church attendance or biblical knowledge, but it might show up in how they lived their lives. We would hope so, at least.

One area where this question has been considered over and over again in recent years, especially in relation to questions about civil society, is politics. Is the political influence of religion declining? Or isn't it? To hear some observers tell it, the influence of religion has waned very badly—with devastating social consequences. Consider the following statement:

Imagine that in 1959 someone sat on an American TV show and said, "I've had a vision! In the next thirty years, we will

49. See especially, Bryan Wilson, *Religion in Secular Society: A Sociological Comment* (Baltimore: Penguin Books, 1966), 14.

have murdered twenty-five million children in ways too barbaric to describe, sodomites will be parading in the streets, and politicians will be proclaiming Gay Pride Week. Your tax money is going to fund blasphemy and homosexual pornography. It will be illegal for a public school teacher to recite the Lord's Prayer or read the Twenty-third Psalm to her class, but that same teacher will be able to tell your child where to get a condom, and where to get an abortion, without your consent or your knowledge. There will be a cocaine crisis, and we will have mass murders going on in our country." Who would have believed it?[50]

That statement is from Randall Terry, head of Operation Rescue, and he is not alone in attributing the symptoms of a decaying civil society to the declining influence of Christianity. William Bennett argues that we ignore religion at our peril, noting that "much of society ridicules and disdains it, and mocks those who are serious about their faith," and he suggests that civic virtue cannot be sustained without religion.[51] E. Michael Jones, editor of a new conservative journal, writes in more strident tones: "As anyone who understood the founding tenets of this republic could have predicted, the suppression of the influence of religion was followed by a catastrophic decline in morals, and the decline in morals has resulted in a catastrophic increase in social disorder. This disconnection of our democracy from the practice of virtue has persisted to the point where the existence of the very republic is threatened as a result."[52]

These commentators reflect an important aspect of the contemporary civil-society debate which argues, in effect, that civil society is in jeopardy because the current leaders of government, including their allies in the so-called liberal media and in universities, are overtly hostile to religion. As a result, the argument goes, people of faith are either prevented from participating fully and actively in discussions

---

50. Randall Terry, quoted in Martin E. Marty and R. Scott Appleby, *The Glory and the Power: The Fundamentalist Challenge to the Modern World* (Boston: Beacon Press, 1992), 37.

51. William J. Bennett, "Revolt Against God: America's Spiritual Despair," *Policy Review* (Winter 1994), 24.

52. Quoted in "Culture," *Washington Times* (May 8, 1995), A2.

about important public issues or they voluntarily withdraw because they recognize that their efforts will be ineffective.

A slightly different interpretation of the political ineffectiveness of religion has been presented in Stephen Carter's widely read book, *The Culture of Disbelief.*[53] The subtitle of this book—*How Law and Politics Trivialize Religious Devotion*—is the key to understanding Carter's argument. As he explains in the foreword to the paperback edition:

> It is not and has never been my contention that the public square—the place where we debate public policy—is *hostile* to religion. Many observers of our politics, Richard John Neuhaus and William Bennett prominent among them, do make that claim with some force, but my thought is different: I argue that in the public square, religion is too often *trivialized*, treated as an unimportant facet of human personality, one easily discarded, and one with which public-spirited citizens would not bother.[54]

An example of such trivialization would be to take a statement such as the one I just quoted from Randall Terry and say that Terry is essentially a man whose religious convictions do not matter and whose political views derive either from some grandiose desire for power or stem from self-interest, such as a psychological quirk that needs to be vented or a lifestyle that depends on raising money from misguided followers.

Stephen Carter is concerned about the trivialization of religion in the public square because he himself is a committed Christian who regards his beliefs as being perfectly rational and strongly directive of his moral commitments and because he thinks civil society is stronger when people like himself are able to speak up and to be taken seriously, even if they do not always prevail. From a different perspective, one could say that trivialization is similar to Bryan Wilson's understanding of secularization. Wilson would argue simply that in-

---

53. Stephen L. Carter, *The Culture of Disbelief: How American Law and Politics Trivialize Religious Devotion*, rev. ed. (New York: Anchor Books, 1994).
54. Ibid., p. xv.

stitutions in modern societies become sufficiently differentiated that the norms of political (or other) organizations come to be dissimilar from those of religious organizations. To say that public officials or academicians trivialize religion would be to suggest that the former operate according to norms of procedural rationality, science, or disciplinary definitions of knowledge, rather than accepting biblical texts or divine revelation as legitimate criteria on which to make claims about public policy. However one views it, the effect of such distinctions is presumably to discourage Christians from participating in the public sphere.

But the story of religion's influence on American politics in recent decades is mixed. It is true, as Randall Terry, Stephen Carter, and others suggest, that religion has been marginalized from public life by rulings of the Supreme Court and by a kind of public nervousness on the part of public officials to say much about religion for fear of becoming embroiled in controversy and litigation. The exclusion of prayer and Bible reading from schoolrooms is a much-touted example.

Yet, in other ways, religion has been more active in the public sphere than ever before. Until the mid-1970s, election studies consistently showed that fundamentalists, evangelicals, and deeply religious people of all kinds were less likely to vote than their less religious counterparts; since the mid-1970s, that pattern is reversed. Clearly, there has been a political rebirth of American evangelicals.[55] Movements like Operation Rescue itself are testimony to the continued, and increasing, involvement of religion in public life. Moral Majority, Christian Voice, Religious Roundtable, and the Christian Coalition have been other examples. So was the candidacy of Pat Robertson in 1988. Conservative Christians may not have been effective in winning approval for their social policies, but their organizations have been successful in signing up millions of new voters and in drawing those voters into the civic arena. Indeed, the picture of declining civic participation that Putnam and others paint remains deficient if it does not take this political mobilization of conservative Christians

---

55. Robert Wuthnow, "The Political Rebirth of American Evangelicals," in *The New Christian Right*, ed. Robert C. Liebman and Robert Wuthnow (New York: Aldine, 1983), 167-85.

into account. As one Washington leader has remarked in a statement that implies an actual tradeoff between the decline in some areas and new mobilization in others: "The organized Christian vote is roughly to the Republican Party today what organized labor was to the Democrats. It brings similar resources: people, money, and ideological conviction."[56]

But conservatives have not been the only ones to bring religious convictions to public life in recent decades. The civil rights movement, led to a considerable extent by black clergy and supported by many white clergy, stands as one of the most profound of all twentieth-century social movements. The long, persistent, and largely successful campaign against the Cold War and against nuclear weapons was to a great extent fueled by religious commitment. In individual lives, we also know that religious views have a significant impact on political views. Religious conservatism is a strong predictor of political conservatism, for example. And many specific issues—abortion, pornography, defense, welfare—line up along the same axis.

We can understand why Christians of all persuasions have been actively involved in politics. Religious people have a long history of being worried about politics. They know—if they've read the Hebrew scriptures (or British history)—that kings and queens can make or break the possibilities of religious expression. In the United States, religious people worry about government infringement on the right to worship. But we also believe a nation must be good if it is to be great. We may not want preachers in politics, but we welcome preachments, the tutelage of moral and religious principles. Separation of church and state has simply elevated the relationship between religion and politics to a position of lasting and legitimate concern.

CIVIL SOCIETY AND THE MARKETPLACE

But it seems to me misguided to ask about the influence of religion only with respect to politics. Civil society is bounded on one side by the formal mechanisms of government, but it is also juxtaposed to

---

56. Quoted in C. Carr, "The Politics of Sin: Christian and Secular Conservatives Join Forces in a Virtue Crusade," *Village Voice* (May 16, 1995), 26.

the marketplace, differing from both these other spheres in ways that require vigilance lest the distinctive values on which civil society depends become subverted. Senator Bradley is again helpful in drawing these distinctions to our attention. He states:

> Civil society is the place where Americans make their homes, sustain their marriages, raise their families, hang out with their friends, meet their neighbors, educate their children, worship their god. It's in churches, schools, fraternities, community centers, labor unions, synagogues, sports leagues, PTAs, libraries, and barber shops. It's where opinions are expressed and refined, where views are exchanged and agreements made, where a sense of common purpose and consensus are forged. It lies apart from the realms of the market and the government, and it poses a different ethic. The market is governed by the logic of economic self-interest, while the government is the domain of laws with all their coercive authority.[57]

Most discussions of civil society are silent about the influences of the marketplace, except to throw an occasional barb at materialism or advertising. Implicitly, it appears, the marketplace is either neutral with respect to civil society, being an arena in which goods and services are exchanged without apparent consideration to questions about values, or the marketplace is a friend of civil society, functioning better than government and providing the relative affluence on which any good middle-class democracy depends. Yet, there are reasons to believe that civil society may be in jeopardy because of Americans' overwhelming tendency to be ruled by the marketplace.

To be specific, one reason why civic participation may be declining is that the average American is now working a full month longer each year than a generation ago. Moreover, a majority of American women are now employed in the paid labor force, whereas a generation ago that was not the case; this means that much of the volunteer work formerly done by women falls to people who are too busy to do it. In addition, a large number of American workers are employed now in high-stress jobs that occupy them mentally even when they

---

57. Bradley, "National Press Club Luncheon Speaker."

are not on the job, with the result that more people feel the need to relax at home rather than take on the added burdens of civic participation. Especially for those who work with people all day, the last thing they need in evenings and on weekends is more opportunity to create social capital. As Senator Bradley suggests, the marketplace is also governed by a logic of self-interest, which may conflict directly with the value of camaraderie and public spiritedness. If there is a culture of self-interested individualism, as many social observers suggest, it is undoubtedly one that is reinforced daily by the marketplace.

Thus, questions arise about the role of religion in relation to the economic realm. Does religion influence the conduct of economic life? Or has its influence waned? Are these even legitimate questions to be asking? After all, doesn't the economy function simply on the basis of supply and demand? Doesn't trade more or less regulate itself? Aren't moral and religious teachings irrelevant?

That, at least, is what a century of economic theory has tried to tell us. But it wasn't always this way. Consider the ways in which religion has influenced the marketplace at various times in American history. In the colonial period, it was not uncommon for clergy to impose sanctions on merchants who charged too much for their wares, and, although business leaders often scorned the advice of clergy, it was common throughout most of American history for business leaders to demonstrate their civic virtue by participating actively in local congregations. But things have changed. Michael Milken, Ivan Boesky, Charles Keating, and a host of others are testimony to that. Sure, they have been pilloried in some religious periodicals. But the power of religion to do anything active in curbing greed seems largely to be a thing of the past.

Let me pin that down more precisely. The Judeo-Christian tradition is, of course, replete with teachings against greed. From the story of Cain, to the story of Abraham and Lot, to the warnings of Jeremiah and Micah, the Hebrew scriptures provide ample evidence of greed's dangers. Jesus' teaching about the impossibility of serving God and mammon and his advice to the rich young ruler, "Go and sell all that you have," carry on the same tradition.

These teachings have not been entirely lost on the American public. In a survey I conducted several years ago of the U.S. labor force, 71 percent agreed with the statement "being greedy is a sin against

God."[58] But how much of a difference does this belief make? Perhaps the news isn't all bad. In the same survey 89 percent agreed with the statement "our society is much too materialistic." And the religiously involved were more likely to say this than the uninvolved. But the study also showed the following: 76 percent said having money gives them a good feeling about themselves; 84 percent wished they had more money than they do; 78 percent said that having a beautiful home, a new car, and other nice things was important to them; and religiously active people gave virtually the same responses as people who were not religiously oriented at all.

In large measure, these results illustrate the human capacity to compartmentalize. We are well trained at putting our faith in one mental box and our finances in another. In fact, 68 percent of the same people agreed that "money is one thing, morals and values are completely separate."

But that is not the only thing going on. Quite a number of people also claim that the Bible offers important teachings about money and say they think about the connection between their faith and their finances. Apparently, though, they are not thinking about biblical admonitions against greed and materialism. In fact, we asked people if they had ever been taught (by anyone) that wanting a lot of money was wrong. Only 12 percent said they had.

One might also wonder just how much the churches are addressing economic issues. Surely every preacher gives a sermon on stewardship at least once a year. This would be a ripe occasion to communicate religious teachings about greed and materialism. But among all church members, only 40 percent claim to have heard a sermon about stewardship in the last year. Thus, it is not surprising that only 30 percent of all church members say the idea of stewardship is meaningful to them. And what it means seems to vary a lot, running the gamut of vague generalities from appreciating God's creation, to using one's talents wisely, to protecting the planet.

Perhaps money is just an especially difficult issue for pastors to address. But the study also considered a variety of other economic issues—dealing with work, business ethics, consumer behavior, and

---

58. The results of this survey were reported in Wuthnow, *God and Mammon in America*.

attitudes toward economic justice and the poor—and on none of these issues was the influence of religious commitment very powerful. To be sure, it did make some difference, for example, in helping people cope with stress at work, or in encouraging them to work hard and to be ethical in their business dealings. And yet, it did not appear that religion was having much of an impact in curbing the economic excesses that may be undermining civil society.

Maybe it was always this way. Certainly people have been tempted to separate their faith from their finances. But there are also many reasons to believe these temptations are more severe in our own society than ever before. Economists tell us that rational, efficient choices are all that matters. Advertisers teach us to compare brands, not to think whether we need something in the first place. Clergy instruct us to be thankful and give freely but consider it dangerous to say much more. In this sense, then, the waning influence of religion in American public life is very much in evidence.

SMALL GROUPS

But I do not want to end on such a dour note. There is also a brighter side, yet another story to tell. That is the story of small groups. As background, think for a moment about the way religious teachings are normally transmitted in our society. At one time, they were transmitted in tightly bounded communities. Till the end of the nineteenth century, the average congregation numbered only about eighty people. Most of those eighty people attended every Sunday, lived in the same community and saw each other during the week, and their children usually grew up in the congregation and generally continued attending it as adults. Under such circumstances, the congregation could indeed be a vital source of social capital from which civic engagement could be mobilized because people met regularly with people they knew well and who generally shared the same neighborhood and lived in similar economic situations.

Things are very different today. The average church member belongs to a congregation of three hundred to five hundred people; megachurches numbering in excess of a thousand members are increasingly common, in fact, now representing about one church member in five. The average church member is thus exposed to sermons as part of a large audience, where paying attention may be a significant problem. Only about one in three, moreover, attend every week; the majority skip about as often as they attend. It is increasingly rare for these people's children to attend the same church; in fact, a majority will not even stay in the same denomination. Churches, of course, still talk of themselves as communities. But if it takes community to make religious beliefs stick and to nurture social capital, these are not the sorts of communities likely to be very effective. Indeed, one might conclude that the decline in religion as a source of social capital is even more serious than Robert Putnam suggests, because people may be going to church as often as in the past but doing so without developing personal relationships with other members. Rather than viewing the congregation as a town hall, where important issues are discussed publicly, it might be better to think of the congregation as a movie theater or sports arena, with atomized individuals sitting next to one another, sharing the same spectacle, but seldom interacting directly.

This is why the small-group movement is becoming so important. Growing numbers of people are finding they need the intense, intimate community that large religious congregations no longer provide. These people are not especially lonely or isolated from friends and acquaintances in their neighborhoods. But they want people with whom they can discuss their values and to whom they can demonstrate genuine caring. They want a place to grow in their spirituality.

The number of people involved in small groups is already staggering. In a national survey I conducted a few years ago, four people in ten said they were currently in some kind of small group that met regularly and provided care and support for its members.[59] Interestingly enough, the traditional Sunday school class is still one of the most common kinds of support groups. About a quarter of all group members fall into this category. Another quarter describe their group as a Bible study or prayer fellowship. Thus, about half of all small groups have an explicit religious focus. Another quarter are best described as self-help groups, of which Alcoholics Anonymous, ACOA, Al-Anon, and other twelve-step or recovery groups are the most com-

---

59. Robert Wuthnow, *Sharing the Journey: Support Groups and America's New Quest for Community* (New York: Free Press, 1994).

mon. Many of these, of course, focus on spirituality as well. The remaining quarter are quite diverse, ranging from book-discussion clubs, to hobby or sports groups, to civic groups.

The role of small groups in maintaining or cultivating interest in religion is quite evident in this research. Overall, 61 percent of all small-group members say their faith or spirituality has been influenced by participating in their group. Many members also claim to have experienced specific spiritual changes as a result of their group. For example, 66 percent say they feel closer to God, 57 percent say the Bible has become more meaningful to them, 55 percent say they have more understanding of different religious perspectives, and 54 percent say they have received answers to prayer. Individual testimonies, observations conducted in a number of groups as part of our research, and other results from the survey also indicate that the spiritual development emanating from these groups is often significant.

The research also showed that participation in these groups is not casual. Most members attend as often as the group itself meets—either weekly or biweekly. Most meetings last around two hours. Most involve few enough people (around twenty) that intimate friendships can develop. And most exist over a long enough period (more than five years) that deep relationships do, in fact, develop. If social capital requires firsthand interaction, then small groups are clearly an important source of social capital. Members see one another on a regular basis, are often in contact by telephone between meetings, hear other people talking about the intimate details of their lives, get to know each other's biographies, and overwhelmingly report that they trust fellow members of their groups.

The caring that people experience in these groups is also considerable. According to the survey we conducted, 82 percent said their group made them feel they weren't alone, 72 percent said it gave them encouragement when they were feeling down, and 43 percent said it had helped them through an emotional crisis. Not surprisingly, these groups are also a conduit for members to show caring toward others. In fact, 74 percent said they had worked with the group to help someone inside the group who was in need, and 62 percent said they had worked with the group to help other people in need outside of the group.

Whether or not such groups have grown in numbers in recent years is impossible to determine for sure, because systematic data has not been obtained on them in the past. The sizable number of groups that are Sunday school classes points to the possibility that small groups in churches are not terribly different in magnitude now than a generation or two ago. However, small Bible-study groups and prayer fellowships that meet in homes or in church basements on weekdays—some precedents notwithstanding—are a phenomenon that church leaders began to promote only in the 1960s and early 1970s. Self-help groups, ranging from AA to various support groups for the bereaved or abused, are also a relatively recent phenomenon, owing much of their present popularity to the mental health and encounter movements in the 1960s. Comparing rates of joining and defecting among current or recent members also suggests that the small-group phenomenon is still experiencing at least modest growth.[60]

Small groups are, of course, intensely interested in the personal problems of individual members, prompting some observers to dismiss these groups as a significant factor in the debate about civil society. Certainly, small groups do not provide the lifelong nurturing one expects to find in families, especially because children are often not included in these groups at all, and the members of these groups seldom enjoy the sort of community with fellow members that one might have found in rural villages or in tightly knit ethnic neighborhoods in Tocqueville's time. But most traditional civic associations did not provide this kind of community, either. Men and women joined the PTA because they were pursuing the self-interest of their own families, or they enjoyed lunch once in a while with fellow Kiwanians because they wanted to be known by fellow business leaders.

For their part, small groups actually function just as well as traditional civic associations in many of these respects. For example, 56 percent of all group members report that they have become more interested in peace or social justice as a result of their participation in the group, 45 percent say they have become more interested in social

---

60. See evidence on this in *"I Come Away Stronger": How Small Groups Are Shaping American Religion*, ed. Robert Wuthnow (Grand Rapids, Mich.: Eerdmans, 1994).

or political issues, 43 percent have become involved in volunteer work in their community as a result of their group, 40 percent say the group has changed their attitudes on some social or political issue, and 12 percent say the group has prompted them to participate in a political rally or to work for a political campaign.[61] Members of church-based groups are also likely to be drawn into other committees and asked to play leadership roles in their churches.

Do small groups shape religious commitment in a way that makes a difference even in the economic realm? Yes. In the study of economic attitudes I mentioned earlier, members of religious fellowship groups were compared with others who were not members. Being in a fellowship group had a significant impact on a wide range of attitudes and values, including attitudes toward money, the value of material possessions, and the meaning of work. Those who participated actively in small groups received the social and emotional support needed for coping with the stress they experienced at work, and many of these people were able to talk about their work and money in relation to values that were generally excluded from the work place and the marketplace. Often, the result was that ethical decisions were made with reference to biblical values rather than in terms of self-interest alone. Being in a fellowship group was also one of the key factors encouraging people to give more generously of their time and money to religious organizations.

In many ways, American religion has adapted well to the secular, materialistic culture in which we live. The churches benefit from material affluence, and they often prosper by making people feel good about themselves rather than by challenging them to live very differently from their neighbors. Clergy often express concern about the moral decline of America but then preach in general terms about the problems that other groups are causing, instead of trying to counsel their own parishioners in better ways of living. But religious organizations are also sponsoring small groups in large numbers. There may be as many as three million such groups altogether, with as many as two million serving religious purposes. If American religion is being revitalized, it is through these groups.

They, too, are subject to the influences of a secular culture. Many of them are shallow, providing distractions from the complexities of

------

61. Wuthnow, *Sharing the Journey*, 320.

social life, and little else. Many are quite intense, but focus rightly on addictions and deep emotional needs rather than on spirituality or on generating civic participation. But they do increase awareness of biblical teachings, they do draw connections between faith and the rest of life, and they do provide the support needed for faith to be enacted. They are an important vehicle for ministry in a secular society, linking religious leadership with grassroots constituents in ways that are more intimate than in large congregations, and they are renewing themselves, attracting new members and drawing in teenagers and young people in their twenties, so that they seem likely to continue in the twenty-first century. They may not prevent the waning of religion, but they may well give it new life and in so doing help to sustain civil society.

PERMANENT JEOPARDY

An understanding of civil society requires us to move beyond civic participation and small groups, however. By most standards, the United States still has a more vibrant array of voluntary associations and nonprofit organizations than most societies, and these vital components of civil society are generally better funded and freer of government intrusions than in other societies. Even if civic participation has declined modestly relative to a high point during the 1950s or 1960s, it might well appear unfounded to worry much about the survival of civil society. Yet, in a deeper sense, civil society is always in jeopardy.

The reason is that civil society is fraught with internal tensions created by inherently contradictory impulses that must be kept in balance for civil society to be humanly desirable. In addition to the social responsibilities that are so often emphasized in discussions of civil society, what Ernest Gellner calls "modular man" is also a feature of the modern idea of civil society, and this is because the free functioning of associations depends on individual citizens who are willing to enter and leave them, constantly renegotiating their personal portfolios of commitments.[62] Thus, the question of individual-

---

62. Ernest Gellner, *Conditions of Liberty: Civil Society and Its Rivals* (London: Penguin, 1994).

ism and atomization is always present; it is not that civil society only corrects individualism, but that it reinforces and requires it. Thus, it is inevitable that questions about individualism will come up in discussions of the good society, but we must also look carefully at the balance between the individual and associational involvements. In this sense, we might say that civil society is always in jeopardy because individualism and associational ties are both needed and yet are at odds with each other.

Civil society is also a precarious admixture of unity and diversity. The quest for a single, holistic moral community is part of the modern vision of civil society, causing us to emphasize civic responsibility, identification with the society, the support of familism, and the instilling of individual moral values, all of which may be so important that they are perceived to be in danger when too much diversity is tolerated. Yet, the very reason for a common moral vision is to permit free people to live together amicably despite their differences and without fear of coercive intrusions in their lives by the state. So civil society is inherently unstable, tension ridden, and dynamic. It is subject to competing moral visions that may become unruly or absorb so much public energy that other goals are not pursued.

These considerations force us to recognize that the civil-society debate is itself desirable, for it indicates that people are paying attention to the inherent tensions in civil society. The same considerations point to a more complex relationship between Christianity and civil society than one captured in discussions of civic participation alone. Christians may well become active participants in politics and in other public activities, but that in itself may not be good for Christianity or for civil society. Much depends on the manner of their participation, especially on whether this participation is civil, being grounded in trust and a sense of civic responsibility. Shrill, unlawful or uncivil, and factionalized public participation is at best a mixed blessing for civil society, and on this score, the record of Christianity throughout the centuries as well as in recent years is not unblemished. The question to which we must turn, therefore, is whether or not Christians can be civil.

2

Can Christians Be Civil?

Pundits are fond of quoting Edmund Burke's famous statement that "We know, and what is better, we feel inwardly, that religion is the basis of civil society and the source of all good and all comfort."[1] Of course Burke was speaking of Great Britain rather than the United States, and in the contemporary debate about civil society it is possible to find widely discrepant views concerning the importance of religion. According to Pat Robertson, "The Constitution of the United States is a marvelous document for self-government by Christian people. But the minute you turn the document into the hands of non-Christian people and atheist people, they can use it to destroy the very foundations of our society."[2] In contrast, surveys of ordinary Americans suggest a rather different understanding. Although most Americans claim some sort of religious faith, they are generally convinced that it is possible to lead a good, virtuous life and to behave as a responsible citizen without holding such views. For instance, when asked, "In your opinion, can a person be a good and ethical person if he or she does not believe in God?" 74 percent of the public in one survey said yes.[3] Other surveys show that tolerance for atheists holding public office, teaching, writing books, and so forth, has risen dramatically over the past half century. Thus, the issue is not so much about Christianity being essential to civil soci-

---

1. Quoted in Lisa Coffey, "Passages," *Indianapolis News* (January 12, 1995), A17.

2. Quoted in C. Carr, "The Politics of Sin: Christian and Secular Conservatives Join Forces in a Virtue Crusade," *Village Voice* (May 16, 1995), 26.

3. "Can Atheists Lead Virtuous Lives?" *Emerging Trends* (December 1994), 4.

ety as it is about what happens when Christians do become involved in civil society.

THE RETURN OF PUBLIC RELIGION

As a starting point, we need to consider an argument about Christianity and civil society that runs in a very different direction from (but does not entirely contradict) the one about declining civic participation. This argument emphasizes the growing participation of Christians in public affairs, not only in the United States but also in many other parts of the world. Perhaps the clearest statement of this argument is that of José Casanova in his book *Public Religions in the Modern World*.[4] Casanova usefully examines how Christians in four societies have entered into a new engagement with civil society in recent decades. In Spain, leaders of the Catholic church have struggled successfully against efforts to disestablish it and transform it into a purely voluntary church, managing to maintain it as an established church with considerable influence over the Spanish government. In Poland, the Catholic church emerged from suppression under Communist rule to serve as an important mobilizing force for the Solidarity movement in the 1980s and now has an active voice in the new government. The Brazilian church, under quite different conditions, has also survived disestablishment to become a national church in alliance with the secular state. Finally, Catholicism in the United States after the Second Vatican Council and evangelical Protestantism after the middle 1970s provide further instances of Christian groups learning new ways of playing a role in public affairs.

The U.S. case becomes especially interesting in light of these comparisons. Whereas Christianity was an established national church in each of the other countries, it has always been separate from government in the United States, and its diverse manifestations have resulted in a denominational pattern that encouraged Christians to respect one another even when they disagreed. But denominationalism also meant staying out of politics and thinking of faith largely as a

---

4. José Casanova, *Public Religions in the Modern World* (Chicago: University of Chicago Press, 1994).

private matter. The fact that religious groups have become politically active in recent years is all the more notable for this reason.

Casanova argues that the "deprivatization" of religion poses an important challenge to understandings of religion that have emphasized the idea of secularization. This is a timely argument because it reinforces the view that academics have used such a wide brush in dealing with religion that they have painted themselves (and it) into a corner. Ethnographic and comparative studies, feminist approaches, and discussions of postmodernism all suggest that social reality is more complicated that it was once thought to be. There is reason to take these arguments to heart, and yet Casanova's perspective retains some of the valuable insights of the older literature while contributing a more nuanced understanding of secularization. As he argues, secularization happens in multiple ways, depending on its social location. In the United States, membership and attendance at religious services has remained relatively constant, yet this fact does not disprove the secularization thesis, as some have suggested, because important spheres of social activity, such as counseling, education, and hospital care, have also become more autonomous from religious organizations. Secularization is also evident in the ways in which religious services adapt to consumerist and therapeutic motifs in the wider culture. Casanova's point, nevertheless, is that religion's return to public life runs counter to these other forms of secularization.

In his view, public religion—religious groups organizing themselves and taking an active role in political and other collective activities— is here to stay, an argument that many observers are likely to find credible for at least two reasons. One is that religious organizations have developed the leadership, communications technology, and financial base with which to perpetuate themselves into the foreseeable future. Their fortunes may wax and wane, depending on the political and economic climate of particular societies, but they are unlikely to recede willingly from articulating their claims. The other reason is the shift away from strong, centralized political regimes capable of suppressing religious movements. The collapse of the Soviet Union has unleashed ethnic and regional rivalries in Eastern Europe that have often been organized along religious lines, and these struggles in turn have encouraged religious groups in the Middle East, Latin America, and Western Europe to champion similar ethnic and regional causes. In the United States, the collapse of the welfare state and widespread cynicism about the role of federal government have created similar opportunities for grassroots religious movements.

The return of religion to public life has, however, raised widespread concern about how responsibly its influence will be exercised. Militant fundamentalists who overthrow regimes in the Middle East and violent anti-abortion protests in the United States evoke fears that religious convictions may tap more deeply into mass hysteria and personal passion than even the best democratic institutions are capable of handling. Observers who acknowledge that extremism is characteristic of relatively few people of faith nevertheless express doubt that religious convictions of any kind can be effectively included in public discourse as long as doing so opens the floodgates for fanatical and antidemocratic values to be enacted. Rather than Christianity being seen as a force for social harmony, it is often implicitly associated with Central American generals, wild-eyed preachers, and emotional outbursts of public piety.

When Christians keep quiet about their convictions, they tacitly agree to trust one another and to behave in ways that do not give offense—in short, they behave in ways deemed to be civil, even though they are not actually participating in civil society. But when Christians claim that their beliefs have implications for public policy, it becomes relevant to ask whether they can be trusted to participate fairly and responsibly in civil society.

Certainly, mistrust has been much in evidence. Adherents of one faith distrust those of another faith because they do not understand it and they wonder if spiritual conviction is actually at work or if political agendas are being manipulated in the name of faith. Public officials who are used to governing on the basis of legal principles and common administrative procedures distrust religious groups whose values may not be so easily reducible to those principles and procedures. Some Christians generate mistrust because their convictions are so strong that they seem intent on imposing them on everyone else; other Christians generate mistrust because their beliefs seem incapable of giving them any moral guidance on public matters at all.

The problem of Christians generating public mistrust has a long history. Framers of modern democratic theory in eighteenth-century Europe were profoundly influenced by the religious wars that had dominated the previous century and a half. Locke's emphasis on tolerance and Rousseau's idea of a social contract were efforts to find unifying agreements that would discourage religious groups from appealing absolutely to a higher source of authority. Indeed, the idea of civil society emerged as a way of saying that people who disagreed with each other about such vital matters as religion could nevertheless live together harmony.

The privatism that came to characterize modern religion during the first half of the twentieth century was the result of long-term social processes that gave religion a place in which it could be exercised with relative freedom and in a way that did not undermine public confidence. Privatism meant that individuals could believe as devoutly as they wished and practice their faith as actively as they wanted to as long as they did not intentionally try to curb the rights of others to do the same. It did not exclude religion from influencing public life but encouraged it to do so through the involvement of devout individuals in other institutions rather than through organized religious efforts themselves. Privatism nevertheless depended on a wide variety of free, voluntary religious organizations that could support individuals in their quest for faith and, indeed, that could also represent these individuals in public according to commonly accepted norms. The fact that Catholics were expected to bring their convictions to public life primarily as individuals did not mean, for example, that the Catholic church was prevented from functioning as a voluntary, nongovernmental institution.

Trust that religiously minded people would behave civilly was reinforced by this arrangement because individuals with deeply held convictions were expected to work through established institutions to achieve their aims and because religious institutions themselves were understood to be part of a specialized system of organizations that worked together. For example, a church board might formulate statements about doctrinal or ethical matters, and even participate in discussions of policy matters, but recognize that the special expertise of scientists, transportation engineers, and professional planners was also important.

The breakdown of this arrangement had as much to do with religious organizations' growing emphasis on the purely personal aspects of private faith as it did with any deliberate effort by secularists to marginalize religious organizations. What analysts of privatism found worrisome even in the 1960s was church leaders' tendency to treat faith as a kind of therapy, concerned chiefly with making people feel happy and with adjusting emotionally to contemporary life, rather than linking these concerns with civic participation. As faith became increasingly subjective, it became harder for people to know whom they could trust and, indeed, whether they could trust themselves (as illustrated by Robert Bellah's famous example of Sheila, the woman who invented her own religion—"Sheilaism").[5] Mistrust of others and questions about one's own identity went hand in hand.

When religion becomes so thoroughly privatized that people are no longer sure whom they can trust, one solution is to promote greater social interaction, as is being done by advocates of the communitarian movement and by leaders of voluntary associations. Churches, too, increasingly speak of themselves as communities in hopes of overcoming privatized spirituality. When people interact with each other in these communal settings, they are likely to develop interpersonal trust. This kind of trust gives people confidence that they are not entirely alone in their views and thus, as Tocqueville argued, can participate in civil society. Christians who are members of such communities can answer confidently that other Christians—at least ones like themselves—can be trusted. The small-group movement has, in this way, encouraged Christians not only to become engaged civically, but also to be civil in their engagements.

But communal interaction of this kind is not sufficient to guarantee civic participation that is also civil. Branch Davidians and Michigan Militia are evidence of that. Members may trust one another but give the wider public scant reason to believe that they can be trusted to participate civilly in civil society. Short of such extremes, congregations also fail to promote genuine trust when they are too large or too diverse for members to gain an understanding of one another. Under such circumstances, the fragile trust on which harmony in congregations is built may be fractured when people break their silence and say what they believe or when the congregation's decision to become involved in social issues forces members to confront one another.

---

5. Robert N. Bellah, Richard Madsen, William M. Sullivan, Ann Swidler, and Steven M. Tipton, *Habits of the Heart: Individualism and Commitment in American Life* (Berkeley: University of California Press, 1985), 221, 235.

THE QUESTION OF CIVILITY

A few examples will help us to move from these general considerations to a more concrete discussion of the problem of civility in
contemporary civil society. Consider these three examples, each of
which will permit us to concentrate on an important aspect of Christian civility:

> *Example #1:* Paul Hill, an ordained Presbyterian minister, was
> arrested and convicted in the July 1994 killing of a doctor who
> performed abortions and the doctor's bodyguard. In an inter-
> view conducted by a reporter for the *Tampa Tribune* at the
> Florida State prison, Hill said that he was "acting as a preacher
> of the word of God." Indeed, he entertained the idea of killing
> someone for more than a decade while he was preaching at vari-
> ous Presbyterian churches in Florida. Explaining his actions, he
> said, "Faith without works is dead. . . . I've always been a doer."
> When the reporter asked Hill if he had any remorse, especially
> as he faced execution himself, Hill replied, "I have full confi-
> dence that now as always Christ will be exalted through me,
> whether I live or die."[6]

> *Example #2:* On Wednesday, May 17, 1995, the Christian Coa-
> lition issued its Contract with the American Family, a list of
> proposals that included voluntary prayer in schools and oppo-
> sition to abortion. That morning an editorial in The *New York
> Times* warned readers that "Americans should not be deceived
> by the fact that Mr. Reed [head of the Christian Coalition] has a
> baby face. . . . The Contract with the American Family . . . em-
> bodies a radical vision for regulating the private behavior of
> law-abiding citizens to accord with the preferences of funda-
> mentalist and evangelical Christians." It went on to say that
> "traditional concern for individual liberty and Constitutional

---

6. Christopher Martinez, "The Journey from Minister to Murderer,"
Tampa Tribune (May 13, 1995), 4.

integrity . . . is about to be hijacked by religious activists . . . promoting their churches' social agendas."[7]

Example #3: In 1989, a philanthropic organization with close ties to the Christian community emerged in Philadelphia and over the next five years raised some $500 million for Christian colleges, seminaries, churches, homeless shelters, and other charitable causes. Its founder, John G. Bennett, Jr., was described by acquaintances as "charismatic and deeply religious" and by one prominent community leader as "a splendid Christian." In 1995, the foundation filed for Chapter 11 bankruptcy, claiming that it had assets of $80 million and liabilities of $550 million. An investigation by the Securities and Exchange Commission discovered that the foundation was a classic Ponzi or pyramid scheme, in which investors were promised high rates of return, paid by the contributions of subsequent investors, until the whole scheme collapsed.[8]

The third example is clearly of a different kind than the first two, so let us return to it momentarily; the issues raised by Paul Hill and by the *New York Times*'s reaction to Ralph Reed focus attention squarely on the dominant questions that have been raised in recent years about Christians' ability to behave civilly in civil society.

As religious groups have become more active in the public arena, those who study American religion, as well as clergy and journalists, have been impressed by the growing amount of conflict generated by these activities. The question at issue is whether this conflict is simply good-spirited, partisan rivalry of the kind that makes civil society stronger, or whether religious rhetoric is becoming increasingly outrageous, reaching the point that it exceeds the bounds of civility and perhaps even encourages people like Paul Hill to commit overt acts of violence.

In previous work, I argued that the major line of demarcation running through American religion since the 1970s has become the divi-

---

7. "Prayer, by Order of Government," *New York Times* (May 17, 1995), A18.

8. Karen A. Arenson, "Bankruptcy Case May Cost Charities Heavily," *New York Times* (May 16, 1995), A14; "Foundation Stiffs Charities," *United Press International* (May 16, 1995), electronic text.

sion between religious conservatives and religious liberals.[9] I tried to explain how and why this conflict emerged when it did, drawing on surveys, interviews, organizational studies, and historical research in which I had been engaged for more than a decade. I examined the state of American religion in the late-1940s and 1950s, showing that the division between conservatives and liberals was not prominent in that period. It was, at least, greatly overshadowed by divisions between Christians and Jews, Protestants and Catholics, and among Protestant denominations. I suggested that there were, however, some predisposing characteristics of American religion that would render it vulnerable to the winds of change that were to arise in the next two decades. One was simply the fact that American religion had massive institutional resources; it was thus exposed to the forces that impinge on any large-scale institution. Another was its inner-worldly orientation; that is, it *tried* to be relevant to social conditions. Still another was its assumption that values (religious ones included) should be linked with behavior.

I also traced the changes that American religion underwent during the 1960s and 1970s. I argued that the following were especially important. First, a widespread erosion in the significance of denominational boundaries. This erosion cleared the decks for other sources of religious identification to become more important. It also made the coalitions we have seen in more recent years (say, between conservative Protestants and conservative Catholics) more likely. Second, there was a dramatic increase in what I called "special purpose groups." These single-issue groups provided the organizational vehicles for religious people to pursue particular causes. They encouraged interaction among fellow conservatives or among fellow liberals. I presented data showing this to be the case. Third, the enormous expansion of American higher education in the 1960s and 1970s was another contributing factor. I showed, in fact, that by the end of the 1970s the major social factor distinguishing religious liberals from religious conservatives was level of education. This had not been an important factor in the 1950s or early 1960s. I also suggested, however, that the reason for this "education gap" was not so much higher education itself, but the particular conditions under which this ex-

---

9. Robert Wuthnow, *The Restructuring of American Religion: Society and Faith Since World War II* (Princeton: Princeton University Press, 1988).

pansion occurred. Thus, I predicted that some of the gap would be overcome in the 1980s. Finally, I showed that the unrest of the civil rights movement and the anti-Vietnam-war protests had played a special role in the emerging divide between religious liberals and religious conservatives.

I should add several other points as well. One is that I did not choose the labels *religious liberals* and *religious conservatives* arbitrarily. By the mid-1980s, these were terms that religious leaders themselves were using widely. They emerged in countless in-depth interviews with church people. But above all, I used them because of a major national survey that George Gallup, Jr., and I designed and conducted in 1984, a survey in which five respondents out of six actually chose to identify themselves as a religious liberal or conservative. This survey provided detailed evidence on the stereotypes, misperceptions, and conflictive relations each group had with the other. I was also able to demonstrate with these national data that the division between liberals and conservatives ran through the major confessional and denominational groupings.

I did not, however, argue that the two groups were separated by an insuperable metaphysical gulf that would somehow prevent them from finding common ground or from working together as members of civil society. Indeed, I was able to show with the survey data that some kinds of intimate, small-group interactions were effective in overcoming the differences. I showed that much of the conflict was fueled by the press and by secular special-interest groups. I did argue that each group was associated with a different version of American civil religion. But I also argued that the very notion of civil religion implied certain common religious assumptions. Moreover, both were subject to the same cultural tendencies, such as an idolatrous orientation toward individualism, freedom of choice, consumerism, and technology.

For all these reasons, I saw hope for religious liberals and religious conservatives to engage in constructive dialogue with each other and to animate civil society by participating in it, rather than becoming such bitter rivals that they would have a negative impact on the collective good. In my book *The Struggle for America's Soul* I outlined a number of positive steps that could be taken by liberals and conservatives in their search for common ground and in their roles as civic activists.[10] Specifically, I asserted the value of small, face-to-face groups in which personal interaction could take place. I outlined a theory of language in which "metadiscourse" (that is, a discussion of the terms of debate themselves) could provide common ground even among the parties to deep substantive disputes. I also suggested that people of faith on college campuses—church-related or secular—could play a special role in examining tensions and achieving more nuanced combinations of, say, conservative theological and liberal social agendas, or issue-by-issue programs, or alternatives to the more polarized views being heralded by the mass media.

I remain convinced that those arc ways in which Christians of different theological and political persuasions can mitigate the intensity of their disagreements. But some years have elapsed since I made those arguments. We need to take stock of some recent developments, writings, and research as well.

CULTURE WARS

One development, of course, is that other writers have jumped into the fray. The term *culture wars* has now become a way of describing the current scene. The idea of a culture war emerged gradually in the scholarly literature during the 1980s, sometimes being associated with discussions of a so-called new class of knowledge workers and professionals whose political views were decidedly liberal and in conflict with those of an older, less well-educated elite of business leaders and industrialists. In this literature, the German word *kulturkampf* was occasionally borrowed, although it was clear that the current cultural struggle in the United States was quite different from Bismarck's *kulturkampf* with the Catholic church in the nineteenth century. Increasingly, the idea of a culture war has come to stand for a wide variety of divisive, contested, and often uncivil disputes that threaten the very fabric of civil society in the United States. First used, to my knowledge, in the title of a book published in 1986 about the controversy over public schools, the phrase itself has gained popu-

---

10. Robert Wuthnow, *The Struggle for America's Soul: Evangelicals, Liberals, and Secularism* (Grand Rapids, Mich.: Eerdmans, 1989).

larity in other books about curriculum debates, in books about racial and gender conflicts, and in books about controversy in the arts.[11] It was the focus of a book published in 1992 by William Bennett, the former education secretary and head of a government commission to combat drug use.[12] It gained national exposure at the 1992 Republican convention in Houston when Pat Buchanan—the conservative presidential hopeful—proclaimed that "there is a religious war going on in this country, a cultural war as critical to the kind of nation we shall be as the Cold War itself, for this is a war for the soul of America."[13] After this, journalists seemed to take as a given fact the existence of a culture war. A search of Lexis-Nexis news sources covering the twenty-four months between the general elections of 1992 and 1994, for example, found over a thousand articles referring to culture wars.

At present, there is much concern that the culture wars—either as a reality or as an image of reality—are contributing to the breakdown of civil society. Radio talk-show hosts who ridicule their opponents with terms such as *feminazi* or overt racial slurs and special-interest groups that encourage readers to resist jack-booted government thugs seem to be the main voices in the public arena. In

---

11. Ira Shor, *Culture Wars: School and Society in the Conservative Restoration, 1969-1984* (Boston: Routledge, 1986); Richard Bolton, ed., *Culture Wars: Documents from the Recent Controversies in the Arts* (New York: New Press, 1992); Russell Jacoby, *Dogmatic Wisdom: How the Culture Wars Divert Education and Distract America* (New York: Doubleday, 1994); Elayne Rapping, *Media-tions: Forays into the Culture and Gender Wars* (Boston: South End Press, 1994); William E. Cain, ed., *Teaching the Conflicts: Gerald Graff, Curricular Reform, and the Culture Wars* (New York: Garland, 1993); Gerald Graff, *Beyond the Culture Wars: How Teaching the Conflicts Can Revitalize American Education* (New York: Norton, 1992); James D. Bloom, *Left Letters: The Culture Wars of Mike Gold and Joseph Freeman* (New York: Columbia University Press, 1992); Henry Louis Gates, Jr., *Loose Canons: Notes on the Culture Wars* (New York: Oxford University Press, 1992); Geoffrey H. Hartman, *Minor Prophecies: The Literary Essay in the Culture Wars* (Cambridge, Mass.: Harvard University Press, 1991).

12. William John Bennett, *The De-Valuing of America: The Fight for our Culture and Our Children* (New York: Summit Books, 1992).

13. Quoted in Todd Gitlin, "After the Failed Faiths: Beyond Individualism, Marxism, and Multiculturalism," *World Policy Journal* 12 (Spring 1995), 66.

the wake of the bombing of the federal building in Oklahoma City, Lance Morrow asked in *Time* magazine, "Is Oklahoma City an inevitable descent into violence of the American culture wars?"[14] While the connections among culture wars, religion, and the Oklahoma bombing were certainly tenuous, they were not entirely imaginary. Within days of the bombing, for example, the Reverend Matthew Trujillo, head of an organization called Missionaries to the Pre-Born, described supporters of Planned Parenthood as "low-life swine," adding, "We should do what thousands of people across this nation are doing, we should be forming militias. Churches can form militias today and teach their men how to fight."[15] First Amendment specialist Charles Haynes, a professor at Vanderbilt University, undoubtedly strikes a resonant chord when he observes that "the public square in America is . . . a very angry place" and when he concludes, this "doesn't bode well for the U.S."[16]

The most serious, dispassionate attempt to make sense of the culture wars is James Davison Hunter's book *Culture Wars: The Struggle to Define America*.[17] Hunter examines the rhetoric that has emerged on both sides of recent conflicts concerning the family, the schools, media and the arts, law, and electoral politics. He finds that the current rhetoric draws occasionally on the religious and political language of conflict earlier in the twentieth century, but that leaders in recent years have adopted an abrasive style aimed at inflaming their followers. Liberals describe conservatives as moral zealots, religious nuts, fanatics, fear-brokers, and demagogues. Conservatives charge that liberals are arrogant and self-righteous, treacherous, deceitful, amoral, anti-Christian, and godless. Both sides have been mobilized by organized special-interest groups intent on raising millions of dollars for their organizations and manipulating the media to depict them as valiant warriors in a righteous cause. Instead of relying on rational arguments to get their message across, they stage flag-wav-

---

14. Lance Morrow, "The Bad Old Days," *Time* (May 8, 1995), 73.

15. "Right-Wing Extremist Groups and Their Link to God," National Public Radio (May 2, 1995), transcript 1597-5.

16. Quoted in Ray Waddle, "Expert Asks Americans to Find Peaceful Ways to Disagree," *Gannett News Service* (March 23, 1995), n.p.

17. James Davison Hunter, *Culture Wars: The Struggle to Define America* (New York: Basic Books, 1991).

ing rallies, hold up pictures of dead fetuses nailed to crosses, parade in sexually outrageous costumes, and demonize the other side by claiming themselves to be the agents of truth.

In a second book, *Before the Shooting Begins: Searching for Democracy in America's Culture War,* Hunter examines how the abortion controversy has been polarized by special-interest groups and by the media to the point that it has become virtually impossible for reasonable solutions to be found. Published just prior to the Paul Hill incident, it appears to foreshadow the advent of an even more violent era in the current culture wars. Hunter is convinced that we must recognize our differences of opinion on abortion and other vital social issues, talk out these differences, and pay heed to each other's positions. If we are able to do that, we will have a stronger democracy and a more vibrant civil society. But Hunter is also of a mixed mind about the possibilities of that happening. In the opening pages of his book, he writes: "Democracy is a fragile enough institution that none of us can ever be complacent about its practical out-working—and especially in the context of deep and abiding cultural fragmentation. The danger of power politics (and its attending tyrannies) may be more immediate than we care to imagine."[18] And toward the end of the book, he asks, "Where, now, is the new *unum,* capable of binding together a *pluribus* that seems ever more fragmented?"[19]

What gives Hunter's questions urgency is that he believes civil society is not being torn apart only by the rash words of special-interest leaders such as Jerry Falwell or Randall Terry or the various heads of ACLU chapters. Hunter believes that civil society is genuinely polarized into two competing world views. Instead of singling out religious conflicts as a special arena of cultural controversy, similar to the schools or the arts, he treats religion as the source of the two underlying world views that are now pitted against each other. Indeed, Hunter's argument builds step by step on my own work and the work of others who have been concerned with the tensions between religious liberals and religious conservatives. Although he prefers to label the two sides progressive and orthodox rather than liberal and conservative, Hunter perceives a deep divide in American

---

18. James Davison Hunter, *Before the Shooting Begins: Searching for Democracy in America's Culture War* (New York: Free Press, 1994), viii.
19. Ibid., 228.

religion running along the same fault lines I have previously discussed—one that cuts through major denominational and confessional lines, that has emerged roughly since the early 1970s, that was rooted in the civil rights movement and the Vietnam war protests, that found legitimation in earlier disputes between fundamentalists and modernists, and that has been heightened in recent years by religious special-interest groups. Whatever their causes, Hunter regards the two world views themselves as the most immediate and powerful sources of the conflicts that have arisen over such specific issues as abortion, pornography, and public funding for the arts. In simplest terms, orthodox believers hold to the view that God exists, that the Bible is an authoritative source of divine truth, and that there are absolute standards of right and wrong that apply to everyone, whereas progressives are less sure of the existence of God, convinced that they must seek their own truth from a variety of sources, and persuaded that moral questions must be decided on situational and relativistic grounds.

If Hunter is right, civil society is in more trouble than most observers have realized. What must be talked out is not simply a way to please the majority and appease the minority on contested issues such as prayer in schools but such fundamental questions as the existence of God and the nature of moral truth. The shrill language of special-interest groups has, in one sense, been unfortunate, because it has made it harder to focus on these underlying issues. But Hunter's analysis suggests that even if the uncivil rhetoric of special-interest groups were magically to disappear, the culture wars would still smolder and probably ignite into open flames again. In his view, the culture war is real, and it cannot be escaped; if anything, more people should get involved in fighting it, because only then can some new moral vision capable of saving civil society be found.

BEYOND CULTURE WARS

Here, we must pause, however, for a reality check, asking ourselves whether the culture war really is rooted in two contradictory moral visions or whether the very idea of a culture war grants too much credence to the rhetoric of special-interest groups. There is, in my view, both a scholarly problem and a normative problem in accepting too readily the culture wars imagery. The scholarly problem is that too much of the discussion has focused on media and interest-group accounts of the controversies themselves. Thus, we have the testimony of the arch combatants. But we do not know what the American public at large thinks. We do not know if the public is in fact caught up in some ontological war. We don't even know what the majority of specialists may think about particular issues. Moreover, when such arguments are made by social scientists, they need to be examined critically. Unless such social scientists are professed students of the media, they should try harder to distill research on what the rest of the population thinks. They should also be concerned about the specific social circumstances that may reinforce conflict, rather than attributing it to some Hegelian battle of ideas. It is, after all, the basic insight of contemporary social science that conflicts can often be minimized by understanding the contributing circumstances more fully. Indeed, as graduate student John Evans has shown in a recent paper—in which he carefully examines a large body of evidence from polls and surveys—there is strong evidence of an "ideology war" (conflict over abortion, pornography, homosexuality, and the like), but little evidence of an "ontology war" (that is, little evidence that ideological debates are rooted in fundamental differences concerning the divine or human nature of forces that ultimately govern life). He does find, however, that the ideology war is rooted in status group differences and in interest groups—such as churches, political parties, age groups, and income groups.[20]

The normative problem with the culture-wars thesis is even more worrisome. Who benefits from having the present situation described as a fight-to-the-death war? The extremists, of course. Little wonder that the phrase has been embraced by Pat Buchanan, William Bennett, and Jerry Falwell. Their agenda is quite different from those who argue for common ground and reconciliation in American politics. If one is serious about the role of Christians in civil society, then surely it does no good to trumpet the idea of a culture war.

Fortunately, the invention of that phrase has not been the main development either in religious or academic circles. On the religious side, there have been a number of developments favorable at least to the prospect of reconciliation among differing parties and more civil

---

20. John Evans, "Culture Wars or Status Group Wars? An Empirical Test of the *Culture Wars* Thesis," unpublished paper, Department of Sociology, Princeton University, 1994.

participation in public affairs. One is that judicatories have continued to use rational, deliberative, legislative means for discussing contested issues, rather than resorting to the extremist politics of the press and the political-interest groups. Another is that some special purpose groups have been established with the express purpose of finding middle ground. Another is that churches have been rediscovering their pluralism—even expanding it to include questions about racial and ethnic diversity, about new immigrants, and about the special needs of that most pluralistic of places, the city. Still another is that mainline and evangelical churches have been learning from each other. The former, for example, have declared the 1990s the decade of evangelism and have launched major efforts to invite neighbors to church, rediscover the redemptive meaning of the gospel, study the Bible, and improve Christian education programs. The latter have distanced themselves from some of the extremist religio-political groups, focused energies on church growth, and become increasingly active in social-service ministries. Small fellowship-groups have also begun to proliferate.

Especially hopeful is the fact that some religious leaders have openly denounced the idea of a cultural war and have initiated efforts to provide a forum for alternative perspectives. Charles Colson, the head of Prison Fellowship Ministries and a prominent writer in evangelical circles, observes:

> The real danger is not just bigotry toward one group of Americans but rather a larger question that concerns us all: It is whether this inflammatory rhetoric will so polarize us as to cripple our capacity for what the moral philosopher Hannah Arendt describes as "democratic conversation." Politicians and journalists alike need to remember: Responsible rational discourse, not name-calling, is the key to maintaining the moral consensus on which free societies depend.[21]

In a similar vein, Jim Wallis, head of the Sojourner's community in Washington, an ecumenical, consistently prolife social-justice organization, counsels:

---

21. Charles W. Colson, "Stop Smearing the Religious Right," *Washington Post* (May 9, 1995), A19.

Among many sectors of the church's life, a new conversation is taking place. Dissenting evangelical voices seek a biblical approach to politics, not the ideological agenda being advanced by the religious right. Strong Catholic voices assert their own church's social teachings as a vital alternative to the religious right and the secular left. Many African-American, Latino, and Asian Christians have a commitment to social justice that leads them to embrace neither the liberal nor the conservative program. New voices from all the Protestant churches feel represented neither by old religious liberalism nor religious right fundamentalism. . . . If religious values are to influence the public arena, they ought to make our political discourse more honest, moral, civil and spiritually sensitive, especially to those without the voice and power to be fairly represented.[22]

Religious leaders have also begun to recognize that incessant conflict between extreme conservatives and extreme liberals can result in a weakening of the religious enterprise itself; as more and more people say, "A plague on both your houses." As a Lutheran layman wrote in *Christian Century*, "We are now . . . in the pits of deep trouble, and I've decided that, as it's being defined in today's climate, I don't want to be a Christian."[23] Jim Wallis writes, "Conformity to the old options offered by the religious right or left will not take us forward. Religious faith must not become another casualty of the culture wars. Indeed, religious communities should be the ones calling for a cease-fire."[24]

On the academic side, a widespread rethinking of the assumptions that culture-wars theorists seem to take for granted has taken place in the past five years. Much of the recent work on American fundamentalism, for example, has begun to challenge stereotypes about its social location, its beliefs, and its alleged militancy, dogmatism, and

---

22. Jim Wallis, "Who Speaks for God?" *USA Today* (March 28, 1995), 13A.

23. Quoted in "A Modest Master," *Dallas Morning News* (April 20, 1995), 1G.

24. Wallis, "Who Speaks for God?" See also Michael S. Horton, *Beyond Culture Wars: Is America a Mission Field or Battlefield?* (Chicago: Moody Press, 1995).

cognitive rigidity. As Scott Appleby counseled in his 1995 Rockwell Lectures, "If you think of fundamentalists as too rigid, inflexible, backwater, mossback, hillbilly and uneducated, then you have missed the point."[25] Fundamentalists, in some accounts, now appear to be less a manifestation of some traditionalist world view than creative arbiters of modern rationalism and expressivism. Research on discourse, religious organizations, and the media is also helping us understand better the extent to which conservatives and liberals alike are subject to the forces of secularization in our society.

My own research has also unearthed some new evidence and produced some new arguments that, in my view at least, need to be understood. They do not suggest that conflict is absent in American religion. But they do suggest some ways in which to think about the possibilities for reconciliation. Let me summarize briefly.

1) The division between religious liberals and religious conservatives that I identified empirically in a national survey conducted in 1984 has by no means disappeared. I have conducted several national surveys since then, including one of the adult public generally and one of the adult U.S. labor force. These surveys suggest that even more of the population identifies itself along the liberal-conservative continuum than did a decade ago, and that there is still relative parity between the two sides in terms of the proportions who identify with it.[26] In short, there is still reason to be interested in the question of reconciliation. As I stressed in 1988, however, the liberal-conservative continuum is, in fact, a continuum. People in the middle may lean slightly to the left or to the right. But they are nevertheless in the middle. They provide a substantial resource for efforts to find common ground. In addition, the liberal-conservative continuum is not strictly equivalent to the so-called gap between evangelicals and the religious mainline. Many religious conservatives, for example, are still members of mainline Presbyterian, Episcopal, and Methodist churches. Many are also Roman Catholics who still find themselves more at home in their own tradition than in conservative Protestant churches. Inevitably, there is some switching—especially among

---

25. Quoted in Richard Vara, "Religious Resurgence is Studied," *Houston Chronicle* (March 25, 1995), 1.

26. Robert Wuthnow, "The Restructuring of American Religion: Further Evidence," *Sociological Inquiry* (Fall 1996), n.p.

Protestants—occasioned by the quest for kindred spirits. But there is little evidence that the two sides have simply gravitated toward entirely different religious organizations. Most important, these surveys also show that the education gap that separated liberals from conservatives in the early 1980s has now virtually disappeared. This does not mean that evangelicals and fundamentalists, for example, are attending Ivy League universities in the same numbers as liberal Episcopalians, agnostics, and secular humanists. But it does mean there are significantly more religious conservatives on campuses today than a decade ago. Thus, the possibility of campus ministries effecting reconciliation has become all the more important. And yet, what some have described as a mellowing effect, wrought by believers coming into contact with persons of other views or being exposed to the humanities and social sciences, is also increasingly at work. This effect, it is also worth noting, appears not to be operating simply by making conservatives more liberal. American culture in the 1990s has shifted away from some of the extreme liberal orientations of the 1960s and 1970s.

2) Much can be learned from sources other than surveys as well. In my book *Christianity in the 21st Century*, I have examined, among other things, the question of whether the religious right will be able to keep alive the agendas that it began pursuing in the 1980s.[27] The answer to this question hinges on taking into account many more factors than proponents of the culture-wars thesis do. Questions of leadership, strategies, public opinion, organizational resources, and political conditions all must be considered. On balance, there is ample reason to believe the religious right will continue to be a factor in American politics beyond the present decade. It has, however, entered a period in its own development when the symbolic politics of media manipulation and of extremist rhetoric has become increasingly disadvantageous even to its own purposes. If its performance during recent elections can be taken as any indication, it will increasingly try to avoid the national media coverage that has polarized opinion, often to the detriment of the religious right. Stealth candidates and communication through media over which it has greater control, such as religious organizations and clergy networks themselves, will be more conducive to political success.

---

27. Robert Wuthnow, *Christianity in the 21st Century* (New York: Oxford University Press, 1993).

3) I have concentrated much of my own attention in recent years on the study of topics that might themselves provide areas of agreement among religious liberals and religious conservatives. One such area is charitable behavior. Helping the needy is surely one area on which conservatives and liberals can agree. And, as I was able to show in my book *Acts of Compassion*, they do in fact agree on its value.[28] Both are also involved—about equally—in programs of ministry to their communities, in visiting the sick, and in helping fellow congregants who may have special needs. As I also showed, liberals and conservatives do talk about their reasons for helping the needy using somewhat different languages. Conservatives, for example, may speak of sacrificing themselves because their Lord sacrificed himself. Liberals may be more likely to talk about the good feelings they receive or see charity as a way of making the world a better place. But, clearly, this can be an avenue toward reconciliation. It helps both sides to see that others' needs are more important than their own biases and conflicts.

Another topic that bears on the question of reconciliation is the relationship between religious faith, on the one hand, and attitudes toward work, money, and material possessions, on the other hand. People are interested in their jobs, trying to figure out their careers, feeling various levels of financial pressure, and engaged in saving, spending, and making decisions about consumer goods. Religious teachings are quite relevant to these issues, of course. Being a faithful steward of one's material possessions, or praying about tough decisions at work are examples. In our national survey and interviews with hundreds of individuals, we found that people don't integrate their faith and their economic lives very well. Compared with helping the needy (where religious commitment makes a large difference), attitudes toward work and money are often influenced only a little by religious commitment. Nevertheless, large numbers of people still think faith *should be* relevant to their work and money. And they wish clergy and religious organizations were doing more to draw out these connections. Moreover, conservatives and liberals do not differ very much on these issues. So here is another area where steps could be taken toward emphasizing the common ground.

---

28. Robert Wuthnow, *Acts of Compassion* (Princeton: Princeton University Press, 1991).

4) In my work on small groups, I have been interested, among other things, in seeing if they can foster reconciliation across religious lines. Small groups have the advantage of bringing people together in an informal setting and encouraging them to share their personal views. They can talk out their differences. The format is very different from reading about some scandalous moral episode in the paper, or receiving a direct-mail solicitation from some religious lobby in Washington. Those are meant to polarize. Small groups, in contrast, function (almost of necessity) by finding common ground among their participants. This does not mean, of course, that liberals and conservatives will necessarily gravitate to them in equal numbers, join groups that represent all perspectives, and then work out their differences. But the potential is there. My research shows, as I have indicated, that 40 percent of the U.S. population is currently involved in some kind of small group that meets on a regular basis and provides caring or support for those who participate. That means there are about three million of these groups in operation at any given time. And about two-thirds (two million groups) are sponsored by religious organizations or devoted to spiritual development. Among all group members we surveyed, 55 percent said they had gained greater understanding of people with different religious perspectives; this figure rose to 67 percent among members of church-based groups. In short, many people are being challenged by their groups to think more broadly and be more accepting of others. The research also suggests some of the reasons why. Acceptance of what people say is one of the common norms in these groups. Seldom is there an authority figure who purports to know all the right answers. Love and forgiveness are popular themes. Doctrine is downplayed. Meeting individual needs becomes more important. These needs are often cries for love and acceptance, for support and understanding—needs that characterize people of all religious persuasions.

5) I have been interested, too, in the question of language, asking specifically how much it contributes to misunderstandings between evangelicals and the liberal mainline. Contrary to the culture warriors, I remain convinced that much of the conflict between evangelicals and liberal mainline Christians stems from different traditions and different subcultures, in which the subtle uses of language itself help to define who is "in" and who is "out." In my initial survey in the mid-1980s, I found that many liberals and conservatives themselves regarded the conflict as one primarily of language. In the

Acts of Compassion project I followed up this idea, paying close attention to the language people used to talk about their motives, values, and involvement in charitable activities. There are a number of detailed examples in that book. But a few of the main conclusions include the following: people generally have complex motives for what they do, and they construct stories to describe these motives rather than talking about first principles; their stories are heteroglossic, allowing them to speak with many voices, to suggest motives, but not to identify completely with any one; religious liberals and conservatives do use different words, and sometimes these words reflect different degrees of certainty about the existence of God or about the extent to which Christians can participate comfortably in the secular world, but sophisticated users of liberal and conservative language also know how to translate, bridging out of their own tradition so that others can understand and appreciate what they are saying; and at the same time, both liberals and conservatives are subject to relativism, to norms of polite nonjudgmentalism, and to the values of individualism that pervade our culture. I have also been interested in formal religious language, especially the language of which sermons are composed. One of the chapters of my book *Rediscovering the Sacred* focuses especially on that issue.[29] I suggest there that Northrup Frye's notion of centrifugal and centripetal forces in religious discourse can help us understand the differences between liberals and conservatives. Liberals, I argue, tend to emphasize the centrifugal dimension of religious texts. The meaning at first seems simple, focused, clear, but then closer inspection encourages us to see broader meanings, spirituality becomes more complex, its meanings open out in new directions. Conservatives do just the opposite. The centripetal emphasis in their language takes this form: life at first seems overwhelming in its complexity; meanings are difficult to pin down; experience and thought show there are a lot of dead ends and false pursuits; sooner or later we come to the realization that simple answers are best, that there is a core gospel truth to be understood and applied to our lives. Some of this, of course, does reflect different assumptions about reality itself. But much of it is built into the language. Liberals bash conservatives in order to illustrate the need for

---

29. Robert Wuthnow, *Rediscovering the Sacred* (Grand Rapids, Mich.: Eerdmans, 1992).

more complex answers. In the process, they themselves oversimplify what conservatives are saying. Liberals also use such complex sentence structures, such convoluted language, that their meanings do, in fact, become difficult to understand. To counter that tendency, conservatives sometimes patronize their audiences, insulting their intelligence less with simple truths than with simplistic arguments, sentences, and examples.

Those are some of the things I have been learning from my research in the past few years. But how does this apply to real life? Let me be clear that I am a researcher rather than a religious leader. What I have to offer is not the advice of someone schooled in the practical tasks of reconciliation. Those who have such experience will have to distill what I say, taking what they can and dismissing the rest. It does, however, seem (to me at least) that much of what I have been finding in my research hints at potential applications. Let me conclude, then, with just a few brief thoughts about these applications.

One implication of what I have said is that college campuses, seminaries, and urban churches composed of students and professionals will continue to be a place where there will be a need for reconciliation between evangelicals and liberal mainline Christians, not to mention reconciliation between Christians and Jews, and persons of other faiths. The reason is twofold: evangelicals (fundamentalists, too) are increasingly being drawn into higher education (there are simply more of them on campuses, even secular campuses, today than a generation ago) and, after that, into the professions; and second, many of the organizations to which they gravitate are special-purpose groups—organizations such as Campus Crusade for Christ, Navigators, societies of Christian doctors and lawyers, or various pentecostal fellowships. These organizations help preserve an evangelical identity but may also serve as staging grounds for single-issue political and moral campaigns. The same, incidentally, is true of liberal ministries, only their causes are more likely to be at the other end of the political spectrum. Structurally, then, there is potential for conflict. This means religious leaders must be more vigilant than ever in seeking reconciliation. There will always be voices, of course, that argue against reconciliation on grounds that compromise of principle is only a vice. But principle can be retained while finding other ways in which to promote reconciliation. My point about serving the needy or thinking about work and careers and materialism suggests that parishioners can be drawn together around common concerns, perhaps much of the time.

Fortunately, there are people of faith in colleges and universities who recognize the potential for scholars to play mediating rather than incendiary roles in the culture wars. Nathan Hatch, provost at Notre Dame, for example, writes, "Given the coarsening of public life, the dissolution of family and neighborhood, and the failing ideals of the professions, there is widespread concern that as a society we have lost our moral bearings." But he adds: "Places like DePaul, Marquette, Loyola and Notre Dame are well positioned to mediate the culture wars. Important voices today sound the alarm that American culture is disuniting, fraying, fragmenting. . . . Catholic universities remain one of the few environments where people with deep roots in both worlds [religious and intellectual] comprise a community."[30] What Hatch sees on his own campus is probably happening quietly on many other campuses, Catholic, Protestant, Jewish, religious, and secular alike: "discussions, retreats and activities that challenge students to think about the weighty issues of life, about social justice, and about the danger of self-interest for aspiring professionals." Also evident on many campuses is what Hatch calls "a commitment to the holistic nurturing of students—body, mind and spirit." These efforts are vitally important for giving the next generation of leaders the skills needed to participate effectively in civil society.

My second observation has to do with the role of small groups. The small-group movement, in many respects, started a generation ago on college campuses. Bible studies, prayer fellowships, youth groups, encounter groups—all have deep roots among students. For this reason, many college-educated professionals who live in cities and suburbs have some experience already with these groups. In addition, large congregations have been initiating small-group ministries enthusiastically as a way of promoting fellowship among their members. Many churches, perhaps especially in urban places, are also devoting their facilities to AA, Al-Anon, and other twelve-step groups. The potential for these groups to effect reconciliation is, as I have suggested, strong.

---

30. Nathan O. Hatch, "The Surprising Relevance of Catholic Colleges," *Chicago Tribune* (April 11, 1995), 19.

But care must also be exercised. Some groups can be springboards for fundamentalist politics. But to take a different example: One of the other groups we studied in our project on small groups is a prayer group sponsored by a mainline campus ministry organization. It has been a caldron of conflict. Many of the students are drawn to it because they grew up in conservative religious homes. They come from the more conservative wing of the mainline denomination that sponsors this campus ministry. So they come, hoping for a home away from home, a safe place to preserve their religious identity. But the leader is a "sixties liberal," a highly educated man who wants to challenge students, shake them out of their childhood faith, and lead them to a deeper understanding. The conservative students see him as a secular force, as someone who is undermining their beliefs. Some of them have left in disgust, joining one of the nondenominational student ministries on the same campus. Some of the ones who have stayed, and who are loyal to the leader, now look down their noses at these conservatives. So the situation is not rosy. But several factors are making a positive difference. The group has been looking at itself, gaining more appreciation of these differences, and recognizing that something constructive must be done. The members are now focusing more on a weekly liturgical experience that unifies them. They are praying more and talking more about their personal needs. And they are finding that other concerns, such as gender, cut in different ways, and that serving the wider community helps draw them together.[31] Another group we studied has had similar experiences. It is located in a cathedral church in New York City. Because of its location, it had to embrace even greater diversity than the campus group. It had to deal with racial and gender issues. It had to minister to the homeless and to members with AIDS. The group eventually fell apart, a victim of other strains in the congregation. Yet, for a number of years, as long as it had the active support of the head of the cathedral, it provided a place in which spirituality was nurtured.[32]

---

31. Antony Alumkal, "Small Groups in a Campus Ministry: Shaping the Future," in *I Come Away Stronger*, ed. R. Wuthnow (Grand Rapids, Mich.: Eerdmans, 1994), 251-74.

32. Wendy Young, "Cathedral Nights: A Group in Creation," in Wuthnow, *I Come Away Stronger*, 205-24.

My third point has to do with language. Congregations can provide a place in which to live, that is, to express one's faith, to be a Christian, a Jew, or a Muslim. But congregations are also places to speak. They are awash in words. Many of these words, for better or worse, are about other words. In short, congregations are places of piety, places for reflection, places to hear the word preached. We are encouraged increasingly to make these congregations a diverse, multicultural experience. We are to live among strangers. And, perhaps sadly, that is very much the reality in many congregations. But we are also encouraged to think of these strangers as our brothers and sisters. We are encouraged to reflect on our collective experience. The first order of business, therefore, must be to reflect on our own language. If we say we have no ideologies—as my students often do—we deny the truth. If we say our language contains no biases, we are refusing to see reality. If we are religious liberals, or conservatives, we must reflect critically on our own traditions. None of us sees with divine wisdom, but only through a glass darkly. The second order of business must be to reflect on those with whom we disagree. If we are put off, we need to ask how much of that is simply language. We must also allow people to tell their stories. Only then can we ourselves see the richness of their traditions. If they feel too unaccepted, too ashamed, too stigmatized to tell their stories, then we all lose in the process. Seeking the center does not mean that we necessarily agree, but it does mean that we agree to communicate.

To say that reconciliation is preferable to an all-out culture war does not mean, however, that people of faith must abandon the deep convictions they may have about social issues. Indeed, abandoning these convictions would be tantamount to a retreat from public involvement into the quiet sanctity of personal life such that civic participation would inevitably be weakened. The issue is not withdrawal but participation in a way that maintains civility in civil society. As one positive model, we might consider a recent accord arrived at among some of the major combatants in the struggle over school prayer. Some subsequent pronouncements have raised questions about the effectiveness of this accord, yet it is still worth examining. After lengthy discussions, seventeen religious, civil liberties, and education groups issued a statement that promised to end the "personal attacks, name-calling, ridicule and similar tactics" in which many of their organizations had engaged. One of the participants explained,

"When we differ, and we will, we recognize our civic responsibility to debate with civility and respect, and to engage in constructive dialogue." Among the affirmations included in the official statement were the following: that religious liberty is an inalienable right of every person; that "citizenship in a diverse society means living with deep differences and resolving to work for public policies that serve the best interest of all"; and that "civil debate, the cornerstone of a true democracy, is vital to the success of any effort to improve and reform America's public schools."[33]

This example illustrates three important features of what may contribute to a more civilized engagement between Christians and civil society: first, willingness to come together, as individual citizens or as representatives of organized interest groups, to discuss issues of common concern; second, explicit public acknowledgment of the value of such discussion, when conducted civilly, to the democratic process; and third, specific affirmation of common values, such as religious liberty, democracy, and schooling, as well as endorsement of procedural norms, such as civility and an avoidance of personal attacks, for the conduct of public deliberation.

SAFEGUARDING THE PUBLIC TRUST

Finally, I want to return briefly to the third example I presented earlier—that of John Bennett, who appears to have swindled Christian organizations out of hundreds of millions of dollars. As much as one might decry the uncivil behavior of Paul Hill or the uncivil language of the *New York Times* in its editorializing about the Christian Coalition, we would probably have no difficulty agreeing that outright fraud of the kind apparently engaged in by John Bennett is a supreme example of uncivil behavior in the name of Christianity. In fact, the irony of this event is that its damage was done most severely to those organizations in the public sphere that were trying to promote a moderate course, encourage informed and rational civic participation, and serve community needs as volunteer and nonprofit organizations, that is, Christian colleges, seminaries, independent churches,

---

33. "School Prayer Rivals Vow to Keep Fight Civil," *Los Angeles Times* (March 25, 1995), B4.

soup kitchens, and the like. Whether or not Bennett's own behavior can be dismissed as that of a greedy and hypocritical individual, the damage done to civil society at large was considerable.

But what can be learned from this episode that may pertain to the relationship between Christianity and civil society more generally? There are several important lessons. One is that an occasional episode of this kind is the price Americans pay for living in a free society. Governmental controls over the functions of religious organizations and charities have been relatively loose because the possible dangers of too much control are generally considered to be worse than the occasional fallout from an abuse of the public trust. A second lesson is that civil society is more than personal values and public meetings; it is big business, requiring huge sums of money in order for civic associations to do their work of training young people, keeping constituents informed, and providing social services. Because of its need for financial resources, the civic order is always subject to the frailties of business leaders and is always in danger of being damaged by the self-interested logic of the marketplace. The leaders of religious and other civic organizations need to be as mindful of their tenuous relations with the marketplace as they have been of their relations with government. And third, the health of civil society depends on adequate checks and balances within the organizations of which it is composed. The most scandalous aspect of the John Bennett affair was not that an individual violated the public trust, but that a single individual had been permitted to operate without adequate checks and balances.

This last observation brings me to a concluding point about Christianity and civility. Throughout its history, Christianity has recognized the dark side of human nature sufficiently that the need for a rule of law has been commonly acknowledged. One hoped for the salutary effects of personal salvation but knew that even professed Christians are subject to the same temptations as everyone else and that laws must be instituted to guard against these temptations and that organizations must be put in place to enforce the laws. Yet, in recent decades, a brand of Christianity has emerged in the United States that attaches little significance to the reality of evil, that naively asserts the possibility of Christians leading happy and morally victorious lives, and that more or less exempts Christians from having to abide by the same sort of laws as everyone else. Under such circumstances, episodes such as the John Bennett scandal become all the more likely. Christian leaders find themselves willing to trust someone like Bennett because he is such a fine Christian individual, because they have the word of other Christians that he can be trusted, because they feel a kind of family affinity with him that reinforces the assumption that he will be fair to people like himself, because this family affinity makes them feel uncomfortable asking tough questions about business, because they believe in miracles that defy ordinary assumptions about human behavior, and because they assume there are indeed some good-hearted people out there willing to serve as anonymous donors for worthy Christian causes.[34] Because they assume God is on their side, these Christian leaders are also willing to assume that they can earn 100 percent interest on their investments when people "in the world" are having to settle for 5 to 10 percent interest. With the advantage of hindsight, it is easy to see that Christian leaders should have not been so gullible.

The answer is not to become cynical and retreat from civil society, refusing to raise money for charitable organizations or to give money to such organizations. The answer is for Christians to play by the rules and to do so by establishing the same kinds of institutional checks and balances on their activities as everyone else. Christians may believe that they have a higher morality than that of the corrupt neighbors with which they live from day to day, but when the John Bennett scandal broke, it did so because a person trained in accounting blew the whistle and because a large corporation called its loans and because the Securities and Exchange Commission launched an investigation.

In the end, Christians can be civil, but only if they recognize that their best values are subject to corruption and that they must have institutional safeguards in order to ensure trustworthy performance in the public arena. In addition to the legal sanctions that catch the Paul Hills and the John Bennetts, it is essential for voluntary checks and balances to be used as well. In the past, boards of elders, the ordination and licensure of clergy, and denominational councils have

---

34. Some of these points were emphasized by evangelical leaders themselves; as quoted in Timothy M. Darragh, "Why Christian Groups Were Easy Lure for New Era," *Morning Call* (May 28, 1995), A1, A18.

helped to civilize the social activities of Christians. At present, the national media, direct-mail solicitations, political-action committees, and large congregations under the virtual control of a single charismatic leader provide new ways of being involved in public life. These, too, must be subject to appropriate safeguards so that Christians can be civil.

3

Multiculturalism
and Religious Diversity

In the preceding chapters, I have argued that Christianity can contribute effectively to civil society in the United States by encouraging
civic participation through congregations and small fellowship-groups,
and that Christians who become involved in public affairs must con-
form to accepted norms of civility, rather than succumbing to the
shrill voices of the current culture warriors or violating the public
trust by defrauding it or by thinking themselves to be morally above
the law. In this chapter, I want to consider the challenge posed to
civil society by multiculturalism, asking whether American Christianity is capable of adjusting to the heightened religious, racial, and
ethnic diversity that characterizes our society at the end of the twentieth century. In this context, I also want to consider whether Christianity can elevate the current level of debate about appropriate kinds
of unifying values or whether religious people will sink increasingly
into a kind of defensive identity politics of their own.

THE GROWTH OF DIVERSITY

To gain an initial sense of multiculturalism, we need to start with
some statistics; multiculturalism is, after all, about living in a racially
and ethnically diverse society. In 1950, 89 percent of the U.S. population was white, 10 percent was black, the remaining 1 percent was
mostly Asian, and the Hispanic population was not counted separately from the white Anglo population. By 1990, the white population had decreased from 89 percent to 80 percent, the black popula-

tion had risen from 10 percent to 12 percent, the Asian-American population had risen from less than 1 percent to 3 percent, other races now made up 4 percent of the population, and the Hispanic population, when considered separately, was 9 percent.[1]

Another way to grasp the changes taking place is to compare the growth rates of various groups between 1980 and 1990. During that decade, approximately 7.3 million immigrants came to the United States, up from 4.5 million during the 1970s, and only 3.3 million during the 1960s. In fact, more immigrants came to the United States during the 1980s than in any period since the first decade of the century, and if the twenty-year period between 1971 and 1990 is taken as a baseline, it experienced more immigration than either the period from 1891 to 1910 or the period from 1911 to 1930. Largely as a result of this immigration, the white population grew by a mere 6 percent during the 1980s, the black population grew by 13 percent, the Hispanic population increased 53 percent, and the Asian-American population rose by 108 percent.[2]

What do these numbers suggest? They suggest that about one-quarter of the U.S. population is not white Anglo—and that proportion is getting larger all the time. In many places the diversity is actually much greater. Take Los Angeles, for example: 33 percent of its population is Hispanic, 9 percent is Asian, and 8 percent is African American, meaning that only half its population is of European descent. Or take New York: 18 percent is African American, 15 percent is Hispanic, and 5 percent Asian American. Or consider the population of the greater Houston metropolitan area: 21 percent is Hispanic, 18 percent is black, and nearly 4 percent is Asian.[3] Especially because of Hispanic and Asian immigration, language diversity has also increased dramatically in many parts of the United States. For instance, a national map showing places where at least 10 percent of the population speaks a language other than English at home includes virtually all of Texas, New Mexico, Arizona, and California, as well as large

---

1. Theodore Caplow, Howard M. Bahr, John Modell, and Bruce A. Chadwick, *Recent Social Trends in the United States, 1960-1990* (Montreal: McGill-Queen's University Press, 1991), 493.

2. U.S. Bureau of the Census, *Statistical Abstract of the United States: 1992* (Washington, D.C.: U.S. Government Printing Office, 1992), 10-17.

3. *Statistical Abstract*, 33.

sections of Florida, New Jersey, and New York.[4] School officials in metropolitan areas complain of having to teach children who may encompass as many as twenty to forty different languages within a single district.

In addition to the fact of diversity itself, the effect of immigration in many areas has been a massive reconfiguration of neighborhoods, housing markets, and schools, as well as dramatic change in established local congregations. Consider the fact that in urban Houston 170,000 new immigrants moved in during the 1980s, while 135,000 nonimmigrants moved out. In Los Angeles, an even more dramatic shift occurred: 755,000 new immigrants were added to urban areas, while 240,000 nonimmigrants moved out; even in suburban Los Angeles, there was an immense shift, with 1.3 million new immigrants moving in and 1.2 nonimmigrants moving out. Miami, New York, Chicago, Boston, San Francisco, and Seattle all showed similar patterns.[5] Those who study immigration patterns also point to huge numbers of temporary immigrants, whose mobility is made possible by long-distance telephone calls and airline service. Thus, an employer in a sweatshop in the Bronx can phone relatives in rural Latin America, ask for twelve additional workers, and expect them to arrive in the morning at JFK.[6]

Furthermore, there is much religious diversity: 6 million Jews, anywhere from 500,000 to 5 million Muslims, 400,000 Buddhists, more than 200,000 Hindus, and as many as 13 million people with no religious preference.[7] Altogether, there are now some 1,600 denominations in the United States, 44 percent of them non-Christian.[8] Some of this diversity has also become evident among elites. For example, a study of the religious affiliations of persons listed in *Who's Who in America* found that in 1930, 95 percent were Protestants, but by 1992, Protestants had slipped to 65 percent, while Catholics had risen

---

4. Jon D. Hull, "The State of the Union," *Time* (January 30, 1995), 54.

5. Michael J. Mandel and Christopher Farrell, "The Immigrants," *Business Week* (July 13, 1992), 116-17.

6. Reported by Alejandro Portes in a lecture at Princeton University, April 1995.

7. Barry A. Kosmin and Seymour P. Lachman, *One Nation Under God: Religion in Contemporary American Society* (New York: Harmony Books, 1993), 16.

8. Hull, "The State of the Union," 72.

from 4 percent to 23 percent and Jews had increased from 1 percent to 12 percent.[9] In addition, lifestyle diversity has also increased enormously: more families without children, more single-parent families, more people who remain unmarried, and more gays and lesbians.

Norman Rockwell once captured the religious spirit of America by painting an Easter Sunday church service; it showed a white middle-class couple with two children. That image was fairly accurate in the 1950s. Today, it represents 8 percent of the population. The rest are not in church, or are not married with children, or are not white Anglos.

But multiculturalism is not primarily about statistics; it is about people and their experiences. The United States is increasingly multicultural, not simply because the population can be divided into a pie chart showing more diversity, but because individual Americans are experiencing more diversity and in the process are having to come to terms with who they are. The nature of this experience can be understood only by considering some specific examples.

One such example is Lavada, a middle-class woman in her early 60s. She is a third-generation college graduate. Her mother was the head of a social-work agency and her father ran a small business until it closed during the Depression. Lavada is an administrator in a nonprofit organization where she has worked since completing a graduate degree in psychology as a midlife career change. She is black, a descendant of a West Indian slave and a German nun. She says it has not been easy growing up colored, then as a Negro, becoming black, and more recently becoming African American. Although she grew up in the North and felt privileged to be middle class and to live in an integrated neighborhood, she says it would be a lie to deny that race was an important part of her upbringing. As a girl, she remembers living mostly among white people and not being very conscious of her African-American heritage. But during and after World War II, large numbers of blacks from the South moved into the community where she lived in western Pennsylvania and her father was hired by the steel mill to help the newcomers assimilate. Increasingly, race became an issue. Now, with more discussions in the newspapers and where she works of racial identity and multiculturalism, she worries

---

9. David Briggs, "In the Halls of Power: Religious Affiliations of American Elite Changing," *Intelligencer/Record* (December 30, 1994), A8.

that we are becoming so conscious of our differences that we are going to experience more conflict in the future.

A second example is Suellen, a Korean American in her late 40s, a petite, modestly dressed woman who speaks broken English. She was born and educated in Korea. Her father was Confucian; her mother, Catholic. Suellen was especially close to her mother and misses her very much. She also misses her sister, who still lives in Korea. Suellen and her husband run a grocery store in an all-black neighborhood. They wanted to locate in a different part of the city but could not afford to purchase a store in a higher-income area. Her daily schedule consists of an early morning walk, followed by a morning spent cooking traditional Korean food for her husband, and then clerking at the store all afternoon and late into the evening. She is very involved in her church—a Korean church that holds services in both Korean and English—and it is helping her to assimilate and to have the courage to deal with people who come into the store and sometimes make her afraid. Her minister told her, "At the beginning, you were very, very Korean, but now you're changing. You see differences in people and you understand them." She says, "I recognize that, too. But sometimes I hurt inside."

And then there is George. He is in his 70s, retired, the son of Hungarian immigrants who worked in a cigar factory. When he was a child, the church in the neighborhood where they lived held services in Hungarian, and George attended every week with his family. Now the services are in English, but it is still the same church, the same building with only a few modifications, and some of the people have been going there regularly for at least fifty years. George says it was like a second home for his parents, giving them a place to meet with the neighbors, to eat Hungarian food, and to talk about news from the old country. He remembers church picnics on Sunday afternoons and parades through the neighborhood with everyone waving American and Hungarian flags. The church has continued to be a second home for George, too, especially after his wife died. But he says, "It's becoming more anglicized all the time. Once some of us pass on, who's going to carry on the traditions? Like this one woman in our congregation, she comes and makes homemade noodles every Tuesday, but she has arthritis now and isn't going to be coming around much longer. As our older members die, our traditions will just go by the boards."

Lavada, Suellen, and George live within fifteen miles of each other. They are quite different from each other in their racial and ethnic traditions. Yet each is experiencing the reality of multiculturalism. Their communities are changing and, as a result, they are having to struggle with who they are. And if these three are different from one another, what about some of their neighbors? What about Harold, a Jewish doctor whose father liked to reminisce about the shtetl in Russia and who is nostalgic about the immigrant community in which he was raised, looking back fondly on the turf wars he had with Protestants and Catholics, and yet not fully understanding why his son is living on a reservation in Wisconsin or why his son has come to feel such a bond with Native Americans and their relationship with the land? And what about Lamina, the Hindu Catholic who has recently immigrated from Guyana and is hoping to achieve the American Dream for her children? Or what about Mustafa, a young Muslim man who is trying to be obedient to Allah in an American suburb? All of them are multicultural in ways that statistics can scarcely express.

THE ROLE OF RELIGION

But what does all this imply for religion? Most Americans—at least five out of six—have been raised in some religious tradition, and these traditions have generally been closely linked to their sense of ethnic, racial, national, or regional identity. Certainly this was the case for each of the three people I have been discussing. Let's take a closer look.

Lavada, the African-American woman, was raised Presbyterian and still considers herself one. As a child, she went to Sunday school and church every week, generally at a Presbyterian church that was integrated, and when she went away to college she became active in the Student Christian Movement, which was also integrated. Although she has retained her Presbyterian identity, she was married to an Episcopalian, has read a lot about Catholicism, African-American spirituality, Buddhism, and philosophy. Asked to summarize her religious beliefs, she says: "I'm a product of all the things I've experienced. What I believe is complicated because I'm better informed. Once I understood Buddhism, for example, I could see similarities between it and Christianity." She doesn't go to church much but still considers it important.

Suellen, the Korean-American woman, is also a Presbyterian, having joined with her husband shortly after they were married. She is very involved in her church, much more so than when she lived in Korea, and more so than her husband. Indeed, she takes some pride in the fact that he looks to her for spiritual guidance. Because he respects her faith, he "doesn't put me down the way a lot of men do," she says. The church is virtually all Korean American. She usually attends the Korean language service. She says the church gives her comfort and is a good place to think about God's word, which in her words "is the right thing to know and makes me very comfortable." She says, "I feel like I find myself there." During the week, she tries to put her faith into practice. She prays every day, not just once but throughout the day, because "God has everything designed for me, and he leads me the right way, and I need him very much." She says some of the people who come into her store are "just bad," but she tries to remember that Jesus died for them, too.

George, the Hungarian man, is a Presbyterian, too. His church has deep roots in the Protestant Reformation, calling itself the Hungarian Reformed Church throughout most of its history, but becoming a Presbyterian congregation in the 1950s. As I mentioned, George is worried that his church is losing its traditions. "I try to help out the reverend and the congregation," he says. "I guess I'm giving it a little extra effort, sort of trying to fill the void before the good Lord says, 'that's it.'"

These three people illustrate the reality of multiculturalism even within a single, old-line Protestant denomination. Their faith is different because of the pluralistic society in which they live. Lavada has adapted by becoming pluralistic within herself; her faith is quite eclectic. Indeed, she considers it important to recognize the complexity and the mystery inherent in spirituality. She says, "I think of [God] as a force, as a kind of universal force for good. I don't think of a personification, any kind of simplistic thing, although that's the speech that we have. One of the things we must [do] is recognize the complexity of life, guarding against simplistic speech, because speech tends to simplify for us." She thinks anyone who adopts a rigid belief system is just going to be on a collision course with everyone else. Living in a diverse world, it is important to her to be flexible in her religious views.

Suellen verges on being a fundamentalist; she has adapted by anchoring herself in Jesus and by trying to show love to others. She is comforted by the fact that God knows what is best for her life and that she can pray continuously to Jesus and find verses in the Bible that tell her what to do.

George has adapted by trying to maintain the ethnic traditions of his church. He helps the reverend put on the annual Hungarian festival, even though attendance has been sparse in recent years. It worries him that so many people have moved away and do not come back to visit.

My point is that multiculturalism is a reality that we all experience in our personal lives. If we are people of faith, we cannot escape the fact that we live in a society peopled by a vast array of ethnic groups, diverse racial experiences, and religious traditions. During the past two decades, that diversity has increased as a result of immigration, and it is compounded by the fact that we live in an era of global communication that makes us aware of the differences within our own communities and around the world. Multiculturalism is a reality that must be included in any consideration of civil society.

Individuals may respond to this reality by withdrawing from civic participation, telling themselves that the world has become too complex for them to understand and that all they can do is take care of themselves. But religious groups cannot be content to encourage such withdrawal (even though some churches may do so), for religion is so deeply involved in civil society that it must inevitably respond in some way to the growing diversity of our world. I want to consider three forms that this response may take. One is what we might refer to as identity politics; the second is what I will call pragmatic universalism; and the third, something that might be termed civil criticism.

RELIGION AS IDENTITY POLITICS

The idea of identity politics has emerged in recent decades from the efforts of blacks, Hispanics, feminists, gays and lesbians, and other groups who perceive themselves as oppressed minorities to stand up for their rights. It has, of course, been criticized as a kind of tribalism that focuses too much attention on loyalties to one's own group at the neglect of common values or, for that matter, individual differences. Tom Tancredo, executive director of a conservative think tank in Colorado, writes in this vein, for instance, when he asserts that "immigration and the multiculturalism it feeds are threatening to dissolve the bonds of common nationhood and the underlying sense of a common national destiny, bringing forward the danger of a balkanized America."[10]

Identity politics, nevertheless, is a significant feature of the multicultural world in which we live. It combats majoritarian thinking in the name of greater respect for differences, including formal recognition of these differences. It understands that individual members of minority groups must band together if they are going to combat racism, sexism, homophobia, and other prejudices. Up to a point, identity politics helps to broaden civil society by giving new speakers a place at the table. If it has become wearisome, it is not because the rights of minorities should be disregarded, but because many of the remedies that it has advocated have had unforeseen repercussions or been effective at the expense of rights and privileges enjoyed by other groups.

One of the ways in which religious groups can respond to the growing diversity of civil society in America is by adopting the strategy of identity politics. Of course there have been religious expressions of the broader identity politics in which various minority groups have engaged, such as black or gay caucuses within denominations. What I want to emphasize, however, is a different kind of response: religious groups that assert their own identity in reaction to the values and interests they see rising in social influence. These groups are typically white, often middle class, and take action in the name of Christianity, calling on community leaders to give them greater recognition alongside the recognition given to other minority groups.

One example has received so much publicity that it may already be familiar. In 1990, a group of students at the University of Virginia sought $5,000 from general funds generated by student fees to support a religious magazine called Wide Awake. When the university turned down their request, they sued, claiming that they were being discriminated against in comparison with other student organizations, including a Jewish group and a Muslim group. Robert

---

10. "Letters to the Post," *Denver Post* (May 9, 1995), B-6.

Rosenberger, founder of the magazine, observed: "With the rise of multiculturalism, non-Western religions are seen as cultural and are elevated up, but Christians are second-class citizens. We go to the back of the bus."[11] Rosenberger was clearly in a situation where it was difficult not to be caught up in the logic of identity politics. The university sought to encourage diversity on campus by providing funds to virtually all groups that were organized enough to cause trouble if they were not given due recognition. Although it could have raised money in other ways, Rosenberger's group felt it had a legitimate right to request funds from the university. When these funds were denied, it was a symbolic blow more than a financial setback, signaling to some, at least, that Christians needed to fight back in order to be legitimate players in a multicultural environment. In June 1995, by a five to four margin, the Supreme Court ruled in favor of the students.

Another example took something of the same form. In 1994, San Jose officials ordered that a traditional nativity scene be removed from the city's annual Christmas in the Park display, claiming that the scene was insensitive to the city's non-Christian population. Yet, two weeks earlier, the city unveiled an eight-foot statue honoring the Aztec god Quetzalcoatl, for which some $500,000 of tax money had been spent. Although a group of Christians protested, the federal district court found that the statue did not violate separation of church and state because there were actually no believers in the Aztec god in the area and because the statue could be considered a multicultural symbol honoring Latinos. One irate citizen observed, "I suppose [the First Amendment] should read: Congress shall make no law respecting an establishment of religion except multiculturalism."[12]

It is interesting that in both these cases, advocates of Christian rights chose to define the enemy as multiculturalism. The same tendency has been evident in school board and textbook controversies involving curricular issues. Christians responded negatively because they felt their own values were being threatened by a kind of relativism that was introduced by teaching about the traditions of other groups. One letter to the editor of a local newspaper illustrates this kind of concern. The author observed: "When you begin to define

---

11. Tony Mauro, "Court Mulls Aid for Christian Magazine," *USA Today* (November 1, 1994), 5A.

12. Linda Chavez, "Religious Rights," *Courier-Journal* (December 11, 1994), 4D.

values, prescribe attitudes and promote philosophies of life, you are crossing over into the realm of religion. . . . Isn't this what the high priests of multiculturalism want more than anything, to have its captive audience, our impressionable children, as converts? Multiculturalism's god is diversity. Its hypocrisy is that it is intolerant of intellectual diversity."[13] Thus, it was not surprising that in a recent study of attitudes toward multicultural curricula, one of the best predictors of opposition to such curricula turned out to be religious conservatism.[14]

The potential for a religious backlash to be unleashed against multiculturalism is evident in these examples. It is a real possibility, given what we know about the nativism of such groups as the American Protection Association and the John Birch Society in previous decades of this century or such groups as the Christian Coalition at present. It is also a real possibility because of the numeric prominence that the white majority continues to hold in most religious organizations. Take the Presbyterian church, for example. Nationally, 95 percent of its members are white Anglos, fewer than 1 percent are Hispanic, fewer than 2 percent are Asian American, and fewer than 3 percent are African American. Among clergy, the picture is only a little different: 93 percent are white Anglos, 1 percent are Hispanic, fewer than 3 percent are Asian American, and fewer than 3 percent are African American. In other words, people like Lavada and Suellen are actually quite rare and, judging from official statistics, it matters too little that George is Hungarian for the church to be interested at all. This means that a relatively inclusive denomination, such as the Presbyterian church, can respond to diversity by making a few token gestures, such as organizing a black caucus or a Korean presbytery, but largely go about its business as it has done in the past. Indeed, the reality of congregational life in most Presbyterian churches on a typical Sunday morning is likely to be far less diverse than the real world in which Presbyterians live from Monday through Saturday. As one laywoman remarked, "There's far more diversity at my car dealer—Hispanic and Muslim men selling Toyotas—than in my church!"

---

13. "Letters from Readers," *State Journal-Register* (Springfield, IL) (December 2, 1994), 8.

14. Brad Verter, "Aiming the Canon," unpublished paper, Department of Religion, Princeton University, 1995.

In settings less open-minded toward diversity than the Presbyterian church, the experience of worshiping within an exclusively white, middle class setting can be the basis for a more activist stance against multiculturalism. Like the letter to the editor, Christians may feel that other values are being emphasized too much in the public realm. Richard Neuhaus, Lutheran pastor turned Catholic and editor of the journal *First Things*, has for these reasons suggested that multiculturalism should be approached as part of a cultural war: "We're very much involved in a culture war in America. One form is the insurgency of religion and religiously motivated political activism in the public arena. Another form, on the other side, is the celebration of multiculturalism, which is basically saying that there is no culture—Western or American culture—that is worthy of our adherence."[15]

The Christian role in civil society then becomes one of playing identity politics, struggling to remind minorities that white Christians are still in the majority. The response may be to file lawsuits on behalf of Christian rights or to support national organizations, such as the Christian Coalition or Focus on the Family, that have predominantly white memberships and are known for opposing certain kinds of diversity. It may also be a quieter, simmering kind of resentment that simply makes Christians angry and unsympathetic toward the emphasis they see in the wider culture on racial and ethnic diversity.

The following remarks, which appeared one day on a scholarly bulletin board to which I subscribe on the Internet, may provide a good sense of this quieter concern about multiculturalism.

Americans are amazingly unaware that America is still overwhelmingly white and Christian. . . . Americans overwhelmingly overestimate the true extent of minority populations in the United States. This is also reflected in the racial composition of Public Television, which was lauded by Children Now and most newspapers for "correctly" reflecting the diversity of American children. In fact, with the sole exception of Hispanics, commercial television came very close to the actual U.S. population, while

---

15. From an interview published in "America's Culture Wars," *Rocky Mountain News* (May 7, 1995), 101A.

PBS portrayed from 5 to 15 times as many minority children as actually occur in the population, relative to white children portrayed.

The message then presented figures from a *New York Times* article showing that white children composed 69 percent of the U.S. population of children, but only 35 percent of children on public television, while blacks were overrepresented by 13 percentage points, Hispanics by 8 percentage points, and Asian Americans by 11 percentage points. The message, incidentally, also went on to complain that the jury in the O. J. Simpson trial did not accurately reflect the predominately white population of Los Angeles County.

Everything contained in this Internet message was factually correct, and yet the inferences were wrong. The problem lay in focusing too much on demographic statistics as the sole reality of cultural diversity. As I indicated earlier, the statistics show that racial, ethnic, and religious diversity has increased dramatically, but they do not capture the complex experience of diversity. Read a different way, they can even be used to prove that America is not nearly as diverse as many people believe. It is thus not surprising that diversity, multiculturalism, and immigration have all become controversial subjects in recent years. In the name of Christian values, opponents of diversity can mobilize sentiment that also protects themselves from having to pay the costs of a more diverse society. Indeed, as with so many other issues, the debate about multiculturalism has been deeply tinged by considerations of economic self-interest. Just as immigration was growing during the 1980s, the U.S. economy was experiencing stagnation, causing many native-born Americans to fear that new immigrants were endangering their own jobs or adding burdens to the welfare system that tax dollars could not accommodate. The results of a 1992 survey were revealing. Whereas six Americans in ten thought immigration had been good for this country historically, 69 percent thought the current wave of immigration was bad for the country. Nearly as many—62 percent—felt that fewer immigrants should be admitted in the 1990s than in the 1980s; the same proportion agreed that new immigrants were stealing jobs from American workers, and the same proportion also agreed that "immigrants use more than their fair share of government services, such as welfare, medical care, and food stamps."[16] Economists are now producing studies by the score to demonstrate that immigration does or does not cost the American taxpayer more than it contributes. But it would be unfortunate for yet another issue in the public sphere to be determined entirely on the basis of economic calculations.

RELIGION AS PRAGMATIC UNIVERSALISM

The second way in which religious groups can respond to the growing diversity of American society is by adopting the stance of pragmatic universalism. I use this awkward phrase to emphasize the inclusive orientation that is evident in Christian theology itself, but also to suggest that this inclusiveness is being adopted on practical grounds rather than involving much explicit consideration of its theological implications. The contrast between this response and the one I have been describing is captured in the difference between a brick and a sponge. A brick does not absorb influences from its surroundings easily; if you don't like those surroundings, you pick it up and throw it at them. A sponge absorbs easily; something new appears, and you say, no problem, we'll just soak that up like everything else.

The dominant Christian response to multiculturalism in recent years has been the sponge rather than the brick. Faced with growing diversity, Christians say to themselves, no problem, we can deal with it, indeed, we welcome it. After all, there is a strong tradition within Christianity that emphasizes the universal love of God for all of creation, the equality of believers in the body of Christ, and the idea that there is neither Greek nor Jew, male or female in the church universal. In reality, parochialism and particularism may have been more common, but in theory these ideals have been voiced often enough to remind people that diversity is not entirely an alien experience. As children, many Christians may have sung the chorus, "Red and yellow, black and white, they are precious in his sight; Jesus loves the little children of the world." Depending on their denominational tradition, they may have supported missionary programs to

---

16. A Harris poll, summarized in Mandel and Farrell, "The Immigrants," 119.

bring native peoples from around the world into the church, or they may have contributed to the financial support of indigenous churches, participated in humanitarian and relief efforts, taken pride in the civil rights movement, or resisted American military intervention in the affairs of other nations. All these efforts carry the implicit message that Christianity is a big enough tent to include the diversity that now characterizes the United States.

The challenge has been for religious leaders to promote actual cooperation among various racial, ethnic, and religious groups. At the congregational level, such cooperation has not always been possible because congregations themselves remained relatively homogeneous. Like Suellen's or George's congregations, they were almost entirely Korean or Hungarian, or like Lavada's, they included one or two black families but were mostly white (or in other cases were almost entirely African American). Diversity may have been limited to sponsoring a refugee family from Vietnam, providing sanctuary for a Hispanic family from Central America, or inviting the choir from a black church to participate in a special worship service. The more innovative work has thus been done at other levels; for example, on college campuses, where people of different faiths and backgrounds were actually sharing a common space, through ecumenical councils in metropolitan areas, or in Catholic parishes or at the diocesan level.

Consider the following as one example of an effort by religious leaders to make a real difference in the ways in which Christians respond to the diversity in their community. In a 1994 pastoral letter, Houston's bishops urged Catholics to celebrate Pentecost by promoting multilanguages and multiculturalism in their parishes and to resist the growing tide of anti-immigration sentiment. "The church needs to say that we are a church that embraces all people," wrote the bishops. "It is the desire of Christ that the church embrace all cultures, all languages and ethnic groups." In a diocese that is 45 percent Hispanic, 12 percent African American, and 12 percent Asian, the bishops urged that true diversity is "not simply a matter of being tolerant of others, nor is it merely a matter of accommodation, accepting a temporary difference in the practice of the faith until others are ready to embrace our expression of the faith." Rather, "each person must come to see a positive engagement with other cultures as a means of enriching one's own faith." In addition to the pastoral letter itself, the bishops encouraged parishes to initiate study groups to talk about diversity and to incorporate people in multiethnic discussions.[17]

Especially in metropolitan areas faced with some of the demographic change I described earlier, Christian groups have had enormous opportunities for promoting greater understanding of racial and ethnic diversity. In the San Diego diocese, for example, the first Vietnamese family arrived in the 1970s, refugees who had escaped from Vietnam on a boat and who were sponsored by the San Diego church. By 1990, fully one third of the diocese was Vietnamese, another third was Hispanic, and the remaining third was Anglo. The bishop is struggling to find the right balance of unity and diversity in each parish. He encourages each language group to have services of its own but also provides common study materials and promotes interaction among clergy and occasional multicultural festivals to bring everyone together. Or consider Grace Church in New York City, an Episcopal church near Greenwich Village whose members are mostly upper-middle-class, white professionals, but whose neighbors are mostly nonwhite and who are aware of the multicultural world in which they live. At the school operated by the church, children are encouraged to reflect on the experiences of their parents or grandparents who came to the United States as immigrants. In a room filled with home computers, children write stories and then compare notes to see how their stories differ from or are similar to those of classmates from different ethnic backgrounds. The school also observes Chinese New Year's, Kwanzaa, and Black History Month as a way of promoting multiculturalism, and at a recent forum aimed at stimulating thought concerning the church's programs for the next century, speakers were invited to reflect on the rising influences of Islam and Confucianism as well as on Christianity.

Nor should it be assumed that all such efforts are being initiated by white churches or by ones to the left of center theologically. In 1995, the Fellowship Christian Academy, a private elementary school, began operating in St. Petersburg, Florida. Its leaders, drawn primarily from African-American churches in the city, are intent on giving youngsters an education that is bibliocentric and Afrocentric. Par-

---

17. Cecile Holmes White, "Strength in Numbers," *Houston Chronicle* (May 21, 1994), 1.

ents who are sending their children there say they have grown dissatisfied with the lack of representation of Africans and African-American themes in the public schools. They believe the school will do a better job at being multicultural than the public schools can ever do. The school is part of a larger plan to promote education, entrepreneurship, economic development, and expansion in the black community.[18] In a very different setting, students at a number of evangelical colleges and seminaries are being encouraged to take courses in cross-cultural communication and new degrees are being offered in multicultural education. The goal of these programs is to prepare evangelical Christian leaders who can teach in inner-city schools, provide social services in racially diverse communities, or work in international agencies.

What makes it possible for Christian groups to embrace diversity in these ways is the fact that most of the new racial and ethnic diversity in the United States is still within the domain of Christendom, broadly conceived. The largest share of new immigration in recent years has come from Latin America and from East Asia, and most of these immigrants are either Christians themselves or come from backgrounds that have exposed them to Christianity. The Korean immigration of which Suellen is a part, for example, has been predominantly Christian, including a large number of Korean pastors who fled from Communism to South Korea and then came to the United States. Suellen is typical of the many Korean immigrants who consider themselves more religiously active and more theologically conservative now than before they came to the United States. Latin American immigrants generally have grown up in Catholic settings and growing numbers have also been exposed to Protestant pentecostal groups before leaving their home countries. The largest number of immigrants who do not fit this pattern are Muslims, and the extent to which diversity must fit within the Christian tent is illustrated by the readiness of many Americans to believe the worst about Muslims and to discriminate against them—or to simply treat them as a kind of Christian denomination that happens to have another leader in their tradition, perhaps like Mormons or Christian Scientists or Swedenborgians.

---

18. Lisa Frederick, "Culture, Spirit Get Priority at School," *St. Petersburg Times* (April 30, 1995), 1B.

The problem, as far as our interest in civil society is concerned, is that pragmatic universalism can be too sponge-like to have any distinct impact on public affairs. To be sure, it can be a voice for moderation and inclusiveness, but it often denies the distinctive understandings and traditions of religious groups, depicting more common ground than may be appropriate to any of them. Phrases such as *Judeo-Christian, the common era,* and *the children of Abraham* suggest a least-common-denominator faith that is likely to be objectionable to any party who takes his or her faith seriously. Religious conviction is eviscerated of any meaningful content, becoming a kind of religious esperanto, in which most idioms drop out, if not part of the alphabet as well. God may still be an appropriate metaphor, but Jesus is demoted from divinity to a moral leader, and "supreme being" or "higher power" may be preferable to "God."

Christians are thus able to participate universalistically in the civil society by redefining their faith to the point that love and service are its essence. Their universalism is pragmatic in several respects: they can spread the love of Christ because they assume there are a lot of people yearning for this love, whatever it may be, and ignore the fact that some people may want to be loved but not in the name of Christ; they can invite Jews and Muslims to worship with them on grounds that it is the act of worshiping that counts, not one's understanding of worship; they can advocate voluntary prayer in public schools on the same grounds, especially because prayer is just good therapy that helps calm children so they can perform better on their tests; and they can emphasize the Sermon on the Mount as a set of moral teachings acceptable to people of all faiths, because these teachings help people have a better day and be more successful at work.

In these respects, people whose faith is like a brick may have more integrity than those whose faith is like a sponge. What the sponge approach does not fully acknowledge is that multiculturalism means something more than living in a diverse society. One can live amid diversity by adopting a relativistic, self-interested stance similar to that of the shopper at a food court in the mall, respecting—even valuing—the fact that Mexican, Chinese, vegetarian, and all sorts of other foods are available. That is the stance worked out a generation ago by advocates of religious pluralism. They assumed that Americans could live harmoniously with one another by eating at home most of the time, sampling other menus once in a while, and letting the free market determine what was available. Multiculturalism is a more difficult stance to adopt, especially from a serious religious perspective, which brings me to the approach I called civil criticism.

RELIGION AS CIVIL CRITICISM

To understand what it may mean for religion to function in a diverse society as civil criticism, we need to begin by recognizing that multiculturalism takes differences seriously enough that participation in civil society requires citizens to approach those differences with sophistication. The key words are thus *difference* and *sophistication*. Coming to terms with difference and sophistication will give us a new way to understand how Christianity can be a critical voice, regaining its prophetic role, and indeed suggest a novel way to institutionalize such criticism.

The role of differences in multiculturalism has been usefully portrayed by the moral philosopher Joseph Raz. He defines multiculturalism as "the belief that individual freedom and prosperity depend on full and unimpeded membership in a respected and flourishing cultural group [and] belief in value pluralism, and in particular in the validity of the diverse values embodied in the practices of different [groups]."[19] What he is saying is that one's freedom depends on being part of a cultural group, and that one's group must respect the validity of every other group's values.

If multiculturalism means finding one's identity and freedom within a community, that is music to the ears of most clergy. One thing religious leaders love is that word *community*. It means that people should flock together, finding God in the group, donating their spare evenings to working on church committees, and giving generously to support the church budget. Most clergy would agree with Raz when he says that being part of a community is not inimical to one's individual freedom; they would assert that individuals are truly themselves when they experience the support of their churches. Indeed, Raz goes so far as to chastise secular liberals (with whom he identifies) for looking down their noses at people with religious values. Listen to what he says multiculturalists should reject: "the superiority of secular, democratic, European culture, and a reluctance to ad-

---

19. Joseph Raz, "Multiculturalism: A Liberal Perspective," *Dissent* (Winter 1994), 69.

mit equal rights to inferior oppressive religious cultures, or ones whose cultural values are seen as limited and less developed."[20] That is also sweet music, although it may be sweeter to fundamentalists than to liberal Presbyterians or Episcopalians.

But multiculturalism is also about diversity, and it is more than a polite nod toward pluralism. Raz distinguishes the new view by calling it value pluralism. Quoting again: "Value pluralism is the view that many different activities and incompatible forms of life are valuable." Or, put negatively, it "rejects the belief in the reducibility of all values to one value that serves as a common denominator to all the valuable ways of life."[21] This is the part that may be harder for Christians to embrace wholeheartedly. It means that other groups, including other faiths, must be respected as having integrity, as being workable, even as being true, despite the fact that their values may be quite different from those embraced by Christians.

One implication of multiculturalism, if Raz's view is the right one, is that relativism must always be part of the deal, but that it also must be kept within bounds. This is the part that comes from realizing that one must live within a tradition, a community, in order to realize one's identity most fully. Living within a tradition restricts one's options. It means that shopping endlessly and casually, as if all options were equally palatable, is unworkable. John Hall, a British sociologist who has also written favorably about liberalism, suggests that civil society and diversity should go hand in hand because the latter encourages individuals to experiment and thus to learn and to gain stronger and more effective identities as selves. Yet he distinguishes what he calls "mild relativism" from "blanket relativism," preferring the former because it doubts that a single set of universal rules can be found but recognizes a minimal consensus, such as respect for law and avoidance of violence.[22] Mild relativism is thus similar to what Michael Walzer, another proponent of political liberalism, describes as a consensus of few, but intensely held principles.[23]

---

20. Ibid., 70.

21. Ibid., 72.

22. John A. Hall, "Genealogies of Civility," unpublished paper presented at a conference on "Civic Values and Civil Society," Boston University, October 1995.

23. Michael Walzer, *Thick and Thin: Moral Argument at Home and Abroad* (Notre Dame, Ind.: University of Notre Dame Press, 1994).

In other words, mild relativism is tolerant of differences, but it does not embrace all values as equally right or good, and it rejects a wishy-washy stance toward one's own values, asserting that some of them are of supreme importance.

Another implication of multiculturalism, in this view, is that civil society will be a place of contestation. It should be obvious from our day-to-day experience that this is the case, yet it is easy to regard civil society as an ideal, the attainment of which will be harmony, mutual assistance, and friendly relations with all our fellow citizens. Leon Wieselteir, editor of the *New Republic*, criticizes this idealistic view of civil society—one that he associates with the communitarian movement—as championing little more than a "moist space" in which we can all find personal meaning together. Wieselteir adds:

> The joke on communitarianism is that the democratic disagreement of America is the work of its communities. The great strain on American society, and on its universalist ideal of citizenship, is coming not from individuals but from groups, from ethnic and racial and sexual groups that live and work and scream in the very space between the individual and the government that . . . communitarians exalt. Civil society is a fine place, but it is not a place of peace. The line between pluralism and tribalism is getting harder and harder to see.[24]

In other words, we may have to withstand the nasty business of tribalism in order to have genuine and healthy disagreements about the nature of civil society.

This observation leads, then, to the question of criticism. Religious groups have always held that their position in society should be not only priestly, patting leaders on the back for their wise decisions, but also prophetic, raising the critical issues that others are not confronting. In a totally relativistic view of multiculturalism, such criticism does not happen; instead, people shop for whatever titillates them and let others shop in their own way. The idea of people finding their deepest identity in groups and being willing to fight with other groups comes closer to the prophetic ideal. At least one

---

24. Leon Wieselteir, "Total Quality Meaning: Notes Toward a Definition of Clintonism," *New Republic* (July 19, 1993), 3-4.

group can be critical of another group. Still, it is not quite clear what prevents such criticism from devolving into self-interested tribalism.

An answer that is worth considering comes from Hall's suggestion that civil society depends on dealing with differences in a sophisticated manner. Sophistication can mean little more than pretension, pomposity, a sham; but in the best sense, it implies a trait or style that is rooted in sufficient knowledge and skill that it is respected for its capacity to provide leadership or to serve as a model in dealing with complex situations. Christianity has always prided itself on having a certain element of sophistication, especially when it was the oldest kid on the block, or when it could claim to be the absolute, universally valid revelation of God. Indeed, it was in this sense that Christianity thought of itself as a civilizing element in modern societies. Being civilized meant having received some type of moral education that was spiritually uplifting, conducive to the formation of character, and perhaps even intellectually edifying. The benevolent societies of the nineteenth century, as well as the Sunday school movement, many missionary efforts, and the settlement house movement, were all attempts—spearheaded in most cases by middle-class Christians— to bring civilization to those in the world who appeared lacking in such values.

In the present milieu, it is harder to know whether Christianity can be sophisticated, especially when it so often succumbs to the foibles of the marketplace, encouraging mindless shopping rather than serious devotion and service. Intellectual postmodernism adds to our uneasiness with projects aimed at bringing sophistication to diverse, indigenous, and disadvantaged peoples. In its extreme formulations, postmodernism denies the existence of absolute standards of truth or of aesthetic evaluation and charges that all such promotional efforts must "come clean" with respect to their own agendas, interests, and perspectives.

In a relativistic world, Christianity may have to be sophisticated in the same way that art or music or the theater are sophisticated, not by claiming to be the unique expression of divine truth, but by somehow convincing its audiences that they have been close to greatness when they have participated in it.

This view of sophistication may seem demeaning when imposed on religion, but I want to develop it as a way of thinking some new thoughts about criticism. In fact, I want to suggest that the way in which people judge art to be sophisticated is by its willingness to be subjected to criticism, which in turn is taken seriously, even if it is known to have flaws. The role of the critic as mediator must especially be kept in mind. If values are neither clearly understood by everyone as being more or less conducive to civil society, and if they are not built into social interests, they must be mediated. The critic in music and art worlds plays an important function by comparing performances, opening up discussions about them, and bringing evaluative criteria specifically to bear on them.[25] Matthew Arnold defined the critic's role very much in this way: "Simply to know the best that is known and thought in the world, and by in its turn making this known, to create a current of fresh and true ideas."[26] In other words, the critic helps people to know whether or not something is worthy, an artistic expression that stands above its competitors, and the critic extends our understanding and appreciation of what we have observed.

But critics cannot function effectively in a vacuum. Audiences and producers must recognize them as playing a legitimate role. Audiences must be trained, and critics must have some institutional base, such as periodicals, awards, and rating schemes. Critics enhance the status of some performers and diminish that of others. Audiences and performers alike accord them respect, granting them the right to make judgments. Criticism is thus more than the occasional notice in the newspaper of an upcoming event, and it is more than the casual "two thumbs up" pronouncement that so often passes for a serious review. Criticism is not negation or an alternative point of view of the kind institutionalized in two-party politics or the American system of trial by jury. Criticism is a searching examination of an artistic or cultural performance that includes understanding it, scrutinizing it from one or more alternative perspectives, and then suggesting new directions for thought and exploration. The critic is a role that peers who are competent as producers themselves may play, but it is a different role from artistic performance, one that must be recog-

---

25. My understanding of the critic derives largely from Wesley Monroe Shrum, Jr., *Fringe and Fortune: Critics in High and Popular Art* (Princeton: Princeton University Press, 1996).

26. Matthew Arnold, *Essays in Criticism: First Series* (London: Macmillan, 1905), pp. 18-19.

nized as a legitimate and independent contribution to the cultural enterprise. When performers grant such critics the right to make a difference in how they are viewed and in how rewards are allocated, their performances take on the characteristics of high or civilized culture. When performances are not judged in this manner but are evaluated strictly in terms of mass market appeal, they are generally considered to be popular or low-brow culture. A mark of sophistication is thus the capacity to withstand the scrutiny of knowledgeable critics.

The religious world has never been devoid of criticism, even in this sense of the word. Theologians have written critical reviews of one another's work; newspapers, more so in the past than today, provided reviews of sermons or of statements by religious leaders; and in recent years, some efforts have been made to provide published guides to local churches, similar to restaurant guides or tourist books. Claims of direct, divine revelation work against the role of the critic, who may be perceived as applying human standards to judge truth that is not subject to such standards. Nevertheless, religious organizations have always utilized some form of criticism as a way of curbing the excesses of those who may claim to have unique access to divine truth.

What I am suggesting is that criticism as a distinct aspect of the religious enterprise may need to receive even more attention than it has in the past, especially now that religious discourse is subject to the influences of mass markets. Criticism should, of course, be distinguished from the most common mode of religious discourse, the sermon, which is more like a performance than an act of self-conscious criticism. The sermon is typically understood as an exegetical exercise, performed orally in the same manner that a commentary is performed in writing. Preaching a sermon involves explaining what a biblical text means and, with the current popularity of narrative preaching, often consists of a retelling or narrative interpretation. The preacher is thus a performer, like an actor in a play, and cannot in the same context be expected to serve as a critic. Criticism enters into many sermons, especially when evaluative remarks are included about the popular culture or about other denominations or religious expressions. However, such criticism is generally not directed reflectively at the preacher's own performance. There may be humorous asides, just as there are in some plays, but the critic's role must truly be a separate role for it to be effective.

Criticism is also different from the academic study of religion, although the same people sometimes shift from one role to the other. Scholarly studies of religion occur within disciplines and take their primary audience as specialists in the same discipline; they do not necessarily function as mediators in the way that critics do, either for the wider public or specialists in other fields, such as policy makers or scientists. Criticism draws on scholarly expertise, but it is more directly concerned with civil society, speaking either from a particular confessional perspective or from the standpoint of an outsider whose primary concern is with the relationship between religion and civil society. It is akin to what Reinhold Niebuhr embodied as public theology or, at its best, in some of the work of social scientists such as Robert Bellah and Peter Berger, or in some of the work of public figures such as Bill Moyers or Maya Angelou. Mark Noll, in *Scandal of the Evangelical Mind*, suggests that evangelical Christians could play a better role in civil society if they had a journal of cultural criticism similar to the *New York Review of Books*, and Noll has been instrumental in launching such a journal.[27] This is an idea that has merit, even though its impact may be small, because it helps to institutionalize the role of the critic.

A PLEA FOR SOPHISTICATION

To conclude, multiculturalism in a civil society means that people have to interact more, talking out their differences, or merely talking about them, but at least not resting content with the assumption that everyone is the same. Civil society can withstand greater diversity as long as groups with different values and lifestyles are willing to engage each other in dialogue. But such engagement must be done with sophistication; otherwise, it devolves into name calling or lurid speech designed only to draw attention in the mass market. To be sophisticated, I have suggested, means being willing to give up some control over one's own claims to know the truth, subjecting them to self-evaluation and to the critical commentary of others.

---

27. Mark A. Noll, *The Scandal of the Evangelical Mind* (Grand Rapids,

Index